Memoir of a Catskill Hotelkeeper

Carrie Komito

Memoir of a Catskill Hotelkeeper

Carrie Komito

iUniverse, Inc.
New York Lincoln Shanghai

Memoir of a Catskill Hotelkeeper

iUniverse, Inc.

For information address:
iUniverse, Inc.
2021 Pine Lake Road, Suite 100
Lincoln, NE 68512
www.iuniverse.com

ISBN: 0-595-29092-2

Printed in the United States of America

To my beloved parents, Ida and Henry Fortgang, and my sister and brothers, Tessie, Louis, Morris, William and Irving—and with love to Avodah and Sidney for nurturing this book, and to Kenneth, Michael, Emily, Dara, Anna, Caroline, Tristan, Wyatt and Lily.

Contents

INTRODUCTION 1

PORTRAIT OF THE HOTELKEEPER AS A YOUNG
WOMAN 5

THOSE WERE THE DAYS 20

A DILLER, A DOLLAR 22

WHOSE CHILD IS HE? 24

OUR CHANGING TIMES 28

DENTURES DO TALK 35

OUR CHARLIE: A MEDITATION ON THE DEATH
OF A CARETAKER 37

A WOMAN'S WAY 43

A DOG'S STORY 45

ON SEEKING A WOMAN 51

THE AFFAIR 55

THE PRINCESS 57

STALKING A HUSBAND 69

A FREE HUSBAND 72

MR. MAYS 75

MY IRISHMAN 80

ON AGING 85

MOTHER LOVE 88

A FAREWELL TO MR. McCORMACK 93

A DESCRIPTION OF OUR MASTER OF
CEREMONIES AND MY FIRST CATSKILL
ENGAGEMENT BY MURRAY WAXMAN 96

THE GLATT WOK 100

INTRODUCTION

I am 98 years old. How did that happen? For seventy years Simon Halkin, my former Hebrew teacher, tried to persuade me to write stories. I met Simon at the Hebrew Union College whose School for Teachers conducted classes near Temple Emanuel, on 65th Street and Fifth Avenue, during the early decades of the twentieth century. I graduated with highest honors in 1925. Several years later Simon left for Israel. Thus began our correspondence, which continued through seven decades until at last word reached me that Simon died.

I am not a demonstrative person. However, even though I didn't express my deepest feelings about him, Simon and I did conduct a relatively intimate exchange of letters. Most of my letters focused on vignettes, incidents from my life and work as owner-manager of a Catskill resort. Simon was a well-known poet in Israel, as well as a scholar. He was impressed by what I wrote and encouraged me to continue composing stories.

I knew I would never be a Pearl Buck, a George Eliot, or a Louisa Alcott. I was aware that there are thousands of professional writers and tens of thousands aspiring to be published. I may have been lacking confidence, but I concluded I would be one more person living a fantasy of literary immortality when the reality was I would be writing just for myself and perhaps family and friends. I knew there were more productive ways to pass my time.

I was influenced, too, by a cousin who made a living for a while writing for the confession magazines. She became disgusted with producing what she considered to be trash and decided to give it up to write an historical novel. After years of arduous research and rewriting, she found a publisher. I thought her book was good. However, it didn't make a ripple—no reviews, small sale. I was sure my efforts would be no more impressive.

Several years ago at the age of 94 I sold my Catskill hotel. I no longer had the Aladdin Hotel to which to dedicate my energy. I was never one to sit around and be waited on or pass my time unproductively. So, I decided to take Simon Halkin's advice. I started to write brief stories of people and incidents. Some of the tales were about my family and ventures in New York real estate, but most focused on my long run as hostess, manager, and therapist at the Aladdin.

I showed some of the stories to my daughter and son-in-law. My daughter Avodah is a physician and writer. Her collections of essays have been reprinted throughout the world and widely praised. She also wrote the first e-mail (whatever that means) novel. Her husband, my son-in-law Sidney, has written novels, short stories, books for young readers and a memoir. He has been honored as a teacher of writing at NYU and the New School University. So—when they responded to my stories, I was on my way.

I feel my book serves a purpose. Not only is it evidence of what a relatively novice writer can produce in her tenth decade, but it may be good reading for patients in a hospital. I may be blowing my own horn, but I consider the stories humorous and frequently poignant. Certainly the book evokes genuine memories of the now vanished Borscht Belt. At the very least it would interest Phil Brown and his colleagues at the Catskill Institute. For me, it also serves as thank you and tribute to the memory of my teacher and friend Simon Halkin. Perhaps at a later time and in a more mysterious place, we will get to know each other even better.

Carrie Komito
July 2003

PORTRAIT OF THE HOTELKEEPER AS A YOUNG WOMAN

It was the year 1906 or 1907. My first recollection was of sitting in a washtub in the kitchen while my mother washed me. The tub was made of something like concrete. It was very rough and very uncomfortable. I remember forcing myself to sit in the middle of the tub to avoid being scratched. The kitchen was the bathroom for all of us who were able to fit into the tub.

The second recollection was of finding a new baby in the house. This was the fifth child. Mother had an elderly woman to help her. She was wrinkled and toothless. She wore an old shawl around her head and, as a great many elderly people look repulsive to the young, I would not touch any food she put before me. I remember asking my mother to get rid of her because she nauseated me. I was only five years old and had no idea how necessary she was to my mother, who had other children to worry about. "Soon, soon, my dear. Not just yet; maybe in a week." I counted the days on my fingers. We lived in a four-room apartment and slept in every room, even the kitchen which was the warmest spot in wintertime.

My father was in the paper and twine business and ran a horse and wagon for deliveries. One day he announced that he had purchased a new horse. I was a little upset because when I waited for my father in front of his store, he'd pull up with his old horse and wagon and hop out and pull me up to the seat next to him. We drove to the stable and if the horse were to pick up his tail and let us have it, that was the natural course of things. Did gas from a car smell any better? My happiness consisted of grasping my father's hand and walking home slowly.

When my father got a new young horse, he coddled it with fresh grass every day. The grass was delivered to the store. I remember picking out all the clover and making a bouquet. When my father saw the flowers in my hand, he roughly pulled them away. "This clover is for the horse. It makes the grass so much sweeter. You mustn't touch the flowers!" That was that. The horse's pleasure was more important than mine.

My eldest brother, Morris, was given the task of taking us to visit grandpa and bringing him the soft apple cake my mother baked for him because he loved it. He was too old to work anymore and spent most of his time just sitting smoking his pipe or reading a newspaper. Two of the younger sons were at home with him while my grandmother ran her leather goods factory.

The youngest son, also Morris, had made up his mind to become a doctor and took many jobs to earn extra money after school. He sold cut glass and pots and pans; was a streetcar conductor; sold candy at Lofts but lost that job by doubling the amount of candy when his friends came in to buy. The other son, Joe, took care of grandpa. He bathed him, shaved and fed him, told him funny stories to make him laugh. His tragedy was that while playing with friends they fed him cocaine and he became addicted. When grandma had him placed in a hospital for addiction, these felons made sure to slip him a fix so that he could never be cured. He died at the age of 28 from an overdose.

Once when we visited grandpa, I got bored. I had to do something. There was a trunk in Morris's bedroom and I decided to look into it. There were numerous medical books, notebooks, graphs, pictures of nude bodies. I didn't put the books and papers back in the same order.

The next time we visited grandpa, I again decided to open the trunk and see what pictures I could find. When I opened the trunk, a skeleton's head stared up at me. As soon as I could move, I slammed the cover back and ran to get a glass of water. It was a lesson I never forgot. My uncle must have known that I would pry. Maybe he smiled to himself, knowing I would behold.

My next recollection was wheeling a carriage with one child in it and a child holding onto either side. I had three children in my charge. I doubt if I was more than twelve years old. I wheeled them to John Jay Park, three blocks from my home. I found three hammocks, put a child in each one and pushed until they were asleep. I met some friends there and we played ball, jumped rope and ran around until the children woke up. The East Side Settlement was near the park. We made arrangements to meet at the Settlement House early Friday evening. There, we stood on line until our turn came to get a bouquet of flowers sent by people who grew them in their greenhouses but had extra blooms. Our home always looked more cheerful when these bright flowers decorated the living room and the kitchen. On our way home, we usually stopped at Rockwell's bakery. There was a standing order to give any child who came in a good slice of bread. It was always warm and delicious.

On other days we went for a treat, which tasted even better. Whenever we had a penny or more, we stopped off at the ice cream parlor and got a bagful of broken ice cream cones. The cones were from real homemade waffles that were then turned into cones. Not the garbage sold today, which tastes like straw. We also used to buy lemon ices from the corner fruit stand. Not the fake sorbet of today but real lemon ices made with sugar, lemons, and water, put in an ice machine and hand turned until a crushed lemon ice was formed. We licked every drop.

The other luxury was taking a shower in the local public bathhouse. Each of us brought a towel and soap and a comb. We then sat on benches where about seventy girls waited their turn. Four girls had to take a shower together. We were given five minutes. When the matron pulled the gong, we had to get out, wet or dry. Most of the time we were half dry and finished our toilettes in the street, where we rubbed each other dry, laughing all the while. Who could say we were underprivileged or suffering?

Eventually, we moved into a larger apartment, and one day my grandfather was brought for a visit. He stayed for about two weeks and I had a wonderful time with him. We played cards and I was thrilled when I won. He also told me stories about his life in Europe. He started smiling when he told me how he had met his wife, my grandmother. He was digging graves. When he heard someone screaming he ran to a well nearby, where grandmother had fallen in, and pulled her out. A friendship formed and in time they were married. Sometimes opposites attract. Grandma was loud and boisterous. Grandpa was tall, slim, and quiet. Yet they got a long although he was twenty years her senior.

I enjoyed every minute of grandpa's visit, but for my mother it was extra work. In two weeks, one of his sons came and took him home. I was a very unhappy little girl. I missed the card playing and his stories. When I cried to my mother, she told me to pretend I was playing with him. I tried this but it didn't work. The real thing was much better. It was no fun playing for two hands.

My next recollection was visiting my grandfather at his home. Grandma was never home. She ran a leather factory manufacturing trunks and suitcases. Grandma would stand by a large wooden table and, with a heavy mallet, would cut out the corners for the suitcases. When she got hungry during lunchtime, she would go through the workers' lunch boxes and eat whatever she enjoyed. These workers were from the same town that grandma came from. They understood her and let her choose whatever appealed to her. Grandpa couldn't help because he was too old, unable to get up and walk. He had spent too much time standing while working when he was young and lost the use of his legs. Two sons were at home, and the older one took marvelous care of him, washing, shaving, dressing and feeding him. He always had a funny story to tell grandpa and then they both laughed. They were like two children.

When mother had time she would bake a 'zader' (grandfather) cake, a soft, spongy cake which grandpa could eat—he had no teeth. (I might note here that although he had three grown sons and three daughters, not one of them ever thought of having a false set of teeth made for him.) Two sons worked in grandma's shop. They had money for cars, women, and other pleasures but not one thought of his father with no teeth.

Every one of my relatives lived in modern apartments in Harlem or the Bronx. At that time Harlem was the Jewish Mecca. There were modern hat shops, expensive shoe stores, the most fashionable clothing boutiques. We had to stay downtown where my father's paper store was located. Today that downtown area is the cream of New York.

I didn't live in a modern apartment uptown, but I was determined to enjoy the convenience of one. Nothing stopped me from taking a towel and soap and visiting my aunts who smiled when I rang their bell and called up to them, "It is only me, I've come to visit." They invited me to take a bath when they saw the little bag I was carrying. They knew what I wanted. I always made sure I left a clean tub.

I kept in touch with a cousin of mine named Lillie who lived in the Bronx. She was an only child and her parents welcomed me. I'd stay overnight and was familiar with her friends. On a visit, one of Lillie's friends pulled a car up to the house and we got in. We were now four girls and the driver. When the car drove into the woods, I was surprised and puzzled. One of the girls got out and said, "I'll see you all in a little while." Then she disappeared. My cousin and I got out of the car and strolled around. I looked at her questioningly. She smiled uncertainly and said, "Loretta has a boyfriend and they have no other place where they can meet and be alone together. So they meet whenever possible in a certain secluded spot. They make love there, and we wait until Loretta comes back."

I felt like a parent, worried about Loretta. Her complicated, devious plan showed me how strong the sex drive is, even for adolescents. And it was so easy to pull the wool over parents' eyes. I only hoped that a tragedy wouldn't happen.

No one took us to school to register. A group of girls and boys were invited into Jan Huss Church, where we learned prayers and other forms of worship. One of the boys next to me always repeated the same words when he had to stand up for a prayer. He muttered under his breath, "We all stand up for Jesus, for Christ sake, sit down." That's all he ever said. When our parents discovered we were attending church, Jew and Gentile alike, we were led to register at a regular public school. Now started the education for that one of us who might become president of the United States. In my haste to get to school on time, I only brushed the front of my hair and ran off. My teacher was a diplomat and she advised me, "Don't pull off your hat so fast. It messes up your hair in the back." For a moment I didn't understand her but I suddenly got the drift. I'd have to get up a little earlier so my mother could comb my hair properly. With six children, my mother had her hands full.

The second thing that bothered me was my teacher's fingernails. I used to wonder about them. They were painted red but always looked wet. How could she work with wet fingernails? I was soon enlightened about shiny polish but thought it was stupid. What was wrong with the fingernails we were born with? Only Indians painted their bodies!

I was an omnivorous reader. I loved and read every fairy tale I could lay my hands on. I became familiar with all types of spelling and became the best speller of the fourth grade. Every Saturday afternoon the public library had a teacher conduct a storytelling session in the library. Not only did the children attend but adults, mostly from foreign countries, who had no opportunity to learn to read, also attended these sessions. I believe they loved the stories even more than the children did.

In the eighth grade, when the girls were called on to read, it was torture to our teacher, Miss Wallace, to sit in her high chair and suffer the girls' lack of reading ability. They stumbled over difficult words and Miss Wallace began fidgeting in her chair. She was an elderly, thin, sickly-looking teacher. Her comment to us was, "I do not expect to live to see the end of this war but you girls are bringing me closer to that end." It was 1913. She turned in her chair and called on me again and again. It eased her pain. I read fluently and she was able to relax. She sat back with her eyes closed and nodded in satisfaction. When the session was over, Miss Wallace opened her eyes, peered at us menacingly, and muttered, "Soon my suffering will be over but I want you to leave with my opinion of you as a class. You are supposed to be bright girls but your light is failing. I wish you Godspeed on your graduation. Now it is someone else's time to suffer with you. Good luck!" What a farewell speech.

Years later, when I was twenty-seven years old, I lived on the West side on 142nd Street near Amsterdam Avenue. Across from our house stood a Catholic church. As I was putting my baby into her carriage, I noticed a tall, thin woman come limping along, carrying a cane. As she came closer I couldn't believe my eyes. "Pardon me, could you be Miss Wallace?"

She stared at me and said, "Who are you?"

"I was one of your students when you told the class that you did not expect to live to see the end of the war."

Miss Wallace stood there a moment and gave me one of her wintery smiles. "Yes, God let me live, as you see. Several times I came to church here to welcome my God, but God said it was not time. Today I am sure it is my last time. I have given away all my possessions and look forward to eternal peace with my God, my Father."

"What about the other teachers?" I asked. She answered, "They must be with God already. I used to hear from some of them, but lately I haven't heard a word. Now I must say good-bye to you. I am very tired now and wish you a happy life with your family, something I never had." With that Miss Wallace crossed the street and entered the church. I just stood there in wonder about God's ways!

While I stood there, I was remembering an incident I will never forget. I was a young child at the time and every time I came out of our building, I was greeted by the boys who lived in the building as 'you little Sheeny, you Jew bastard.' I would run back to my mother, hurt and alarmed. "Why are those nasty boys calling me names?" My mother looked at me sadly. "I can't go into a big story now but please don't pay any attention on them. These things will happen now and then. I can't stop this kind of talk. Their parents are teaching them hatred. In the end they will suffer. You have to learn to live with your enemies. Someday they may learn their lesson." I wondered about Miss Wallace's God, and mine.

When I was thirteen years old, I sat in our kitchen, resting on my knees on a chair near our table. My uncle, my father's brother, was pleading with my father "I'm asking you for a loan because I do not have enough money to go ahead with a plan. I've been thinking for a long time that it's a good idea to have talking moving pictures. They will bring in lots of money because I will be the first one to show such pictures." I was listening and wondering how this could happen. The pictures weren't alive so how could they talk? I wouldn't dare ask any questions. In the end my father agreed to the loan which was for six years since it would take time to build a movie and to feature this novelty. "Six years", I thought to myself. "I will be 19 years old. Imagine, I will be a grown up woman."

A few years passed but I never forgot this conversation. One day I asked my father to take me to see Uncle Barel's movie, this wonder of wonders. Who could believe such a simple project? My uncle had a very large screen below the picture, concealing all kinds of instruments—a piano, a drum, a horn, and noise-makers. A couple behind the screen acted out all the happenings in the film. When a woman cried, the woman behind the screen cried; when a man yelled, the man behind the screen yelled. When fire engines ran to a fire, the horns would blow and drums would beat for excitement. The audience loved it and theatre was always packed with people anxious to witness such a novelty. My uncle was in the money and it didn't take long to pay off his debt.

I believe my uncle was the innovator of the talking picture, but no one to hail him as the originator. He died an unknown genius. The method was so simple. My uncle was the first one to test the test.

It was high school graduation time. I knew my mother was a very busy woman with a large family, so I asked my father to come to my graduation. "Oh, sure," he answered. As the appointed time was nearing, I saw my father still working in the store and making no move to wash and dress. I was so exasperated that I cried out, "Pa it is time to get dressed. We'll be late!"

My father looked at me and said "Do me a favor, make it 'anudder' time." I ran upstairs, tears blinding my eyes, and started to weep started to hysterically. My mother stood looking at me, heaved a great sigh and said, "All right, I'll come with you." She changed her skirt, draped one of her shawls around her shoulders and off we went.

At the ceremonies, I was called to receive a medal for the best senior scholastic record. Mother's eyes shone with pride. The teachers came over to us at the end of the exercises and congratulated my mother on having such a brilliant daughter. They paid no attention to my mother's old shawl. They were congratulating her about me. I felt important for the first time. I was a human being who had excelled.

On our way home, we stopped of at a soda stand on Third Avenue and 68th Street. Mother had a 3-cents-plain seltzer and I had a 5-cent egg cream. If we had been at the Waldorf Astoria, I couldn't have been happier.

It seems as if I possessed maternal instincts. It was my pleasure to get up early in the morning before my family and go shopping for breakfast—fresh rolls, cakes, the rich milk from the top of a milk can (no bottled milk at the time) from the bakery next door (friends of my mother). I enjoyed watching my family put away all these goodies. This maternal instinct lasted through my life—sometimes overwhelming me. However, I did refuse to stay at home to help with the housework. I hated the furnishings—just beds, chairs, a dining room table; no soft carpeting or easy chairs, nothing to make life a little more pleasant. My parents were immigrants and their energies were bent on raising and feeding a family. We also had a poorly heated home and I was glad to get away whenever I could.

I hung out the wet wash; folded it when dry; did some ironing; helped scrub the floors by pushing my mother away when she got down on the floor. I brought up coal from the cellar when necessary. My mother never asked the boys to do this chore. Boys were a privileged class to the Jewish people. My mother was an indefatigable worker. She always said that work never killed anyone—but it shortened her life.

My mother taught herself to read and that was her pleasure at night when she was too tired to do anything else. I was shocked one day when she mentioned that she had read *Daniel Deronda* by George Elliot. Many educated people have never read George Elliot.

My first job was with the American Book Company at sixteen dollars per week. When I was questioned about the church I attended, I answered that I was looking for a job which had nothing to do with religion. My questioner was a little disturbed as to how to get on with his questions and he consulted another officer. They were afraid I might have been sent by some government organization so they decided to hire me. I later found out that I was the second Jewish employee in that outfit.

Since I was near Wanamakers at Ninth Street, my first salary went for a lovely tan angora shawl for my mother. It was large and cozy. Mother loved it and wore it for every occasion—shopping, visiting, and weddings. I got sixteen thousand dollars worth of pleasure watching her wear it.

I became a student at the Hebrew Union College School for Teachers. As I was entering the classroom, and before I sat down, my Hebrew teacher, Simon Halkin, glanced up and immediately rose and asked, "What is your name?" He smiled at me and said, "Welcome to my class." In due time our feelings became mutual. Before I knew the meaning of the Hebrew word inscribed at the bottom of every one of my papers—'with love'—I was infatuated with my teacher. I had beautiful auburn hair and a pleasant humorous face, and he seemed to appreciate me. For seventy years we were devoted friends and carried on a loving correspondence until the day of his death. If he had stayed in the United States instead of going to Israel, we might have married. His plea was that he was tubercular; he was rejected by the army for that reason and was uncertain about his life. Several years later he married in Israel.

I had a wonderful time in school and at the end of the course I won the Isaac Mayer Memorial Prize for the highest scholarship attainment. All the teachers were my friends.

I enjoyed my work at the American Book Company. One day I was aware that a special private secretary had left and I felt that I could qualify for the job. Instead, I found that the company had advertised. I saw quite a number of applicants coming in all week. The following week I was suddenly called to take dictation from one of the top schoolbook salesman. His name was Mr. Coffin. He was a heavyset man with a full mustache and beard. He also had a low voice but I had good hearing. I made sure that I understood every word. However, one word stumped me and I wouldn't ask. It sounded like 'oleomargarine'. When I got back to my desk I looked for words that sounded like 'oleo' and found 'oleaginous which meant smooth, oily. Now I understood Mr. Coffin's sentence which read, 'With your smooth and oleaginous way, I am sure you can accomplish the sale.'

As luck would have it, the next day was a Jewish Holiday. I stayed late at the office until Mr. Coffin's letters were finished and then placed them on his desk. "Whatever would be, would be."

When I returned two days later, I was indeed surprised when I was called to Mr. Coffin's desk. He turned to me and said, "You are the first person who handed in all perfect letters; just amazing. You wouldn't believe the rubbish those applicants turned in. Oh well, I'd rather have the Jew than the devil with the holy water." (And that from a big company.)

My job demanded more quality than quantity. Since I had a lot of spare time I started studying my Hebrew lessons at the office. I was copying notes when suddenly my textbook was picked up. There was Mr. Coffin standing by my desk and scrutinizing the hieroglyphics through his thick glasses and asking me the meaning of those figures. Mr. Coffin looked quite impressed and after a little thought he said with a smile, "From now on I shall call you Dr. Fortgang."

For two years I was Mr. Coffin's secretary and we worked together harmoniously. Two years later my mother had a heart attack and that was the end of my job. Fortunately, it was also the end of my course of study at the college, so I was free to take care of my mother's needs.

For two years I took care of my mother until she recovered. I have to mention here (just a note) that I never got over my romance with cream cheese, which helped me a great deal when I was taking care of my mother. Whenever I had a nickel I ran to our grocery store. When the grocer saw me coming in, he had the cream cheese ready and handed it to me with a smile. At that time the cream cheese came wrapped in the shape of a tootsie roll, only much thicker. That was my candy money but I preferred the cheese and would lick it like an ice cream cone, savoring the taste on my tongue. It is still the only cheese I eat. Now you know my weakness and my strength.

When my mother was completely well, my father donated a Torah in her honor to his synagogue, which was in downtown New York. At the ceremony Abe Komito, the cantor's son, was present. After he was introduced to me he never left my side. He courted me assiduously, coming every night from Brooklyn until I accepted him. Abe was a civil engineer (nickname "Honest Abe") with the Department of Highways in Brooklyn. He worked there most of his adult life.

Eventually my husband Abe rose through the ranks to become Deputy to the Chief Engineer. He was next in line for the top job and his colleagues thought him deserving. But not the Borough President. He had a son who, although not as qualified as a civil engineer, aspired to that position. As politics decreed, the man with the political connections got the job.

I'll say this for Abe: he may have been disappointed, even severely insulted, but he didn't complain. He accepted it as the way of the world and went right on working as conscientiously as ever. The man who became his boss was so dependent upon him he rarely signed an agreement, order or contract unless Abe approved and signed along with him.

But it bothered me that my husband accepted being a victim. He stayed on the job. He told me the pension after retirement was his incentive. That pension was like a carrot hanging over the donkey's eyes. I didn't respect him for accepting such a paltry reward after such insult. As it turned out, Abe only lived a brief time after his retirement and the pension was a minor salve for a major wound.

Meanwhile I went on to other challenges, other businesses. The most consuming and rewarding was ownership and management of a summer resort in Woodbourne, New York, heart of the Catskills, also known as the Borscht Belt. That was the adventure Abe Komito shared with me. I'm not sure he always liked it, but he did pitch in, designing and building the indoor pool, assisting from time to time with renting rooms, charming guests and consulting as my deputy.

THOSE WERE THE DAYS

Do you remember when there were more guests reserving rooms in the hotels in the Catskill Mountains than there were rooms to accommodate them? Those were the golden days. You could sell any room. The Catskills were the summer home for Jewish vacationers.

One day I had a long line of people checking in. Towards the end of the line there was a middle-aged man who, together with his grandson, had spent several summers with me. They always had a grand time and the guests used to watch him teaching his grandson to dance in our playhouse. This time he came with no reservation—and a lady friend. When he reached my desk I said to him, "I have only one room left. I don't have another room open." Mr. Klein-that was his name—started to leave, saying, "Sorry. I want two rooms." Before he reached the exit he turned around and called out: "Mrs. Brown (Brown's Hotel) will give me two rooms, but I hate to leave."

I crooked my little finger and called back: "I have a suggestion for you. Come over here and I will tell you." When Mr. Klein returned to the desk, I said, "I have a nice room and I can hang a blanket to divide the room, so it will be like two rooms." Mr. Klein looked at me for a moment and then said, "It's a deal (pronounced dill)." I have used that pronunciation for many years in difficult situations. I checked him in.

I never gave him the blanket and he never asked me for one. At the end of the week, Mr. Klein came stomping down the stairs and over to my desk. "I'm leaving this week. I want you to make out two separate bills. One for me and one for my lady friend."

I looked inquiringly at him and said, "It didn't turn out right? She didn't make you happy?"

"God damn it, she was a real no-goodnick. I can't wait to get home."

Thus ended a country romance. Mr. Klein did better with his grandson.

A DILLER, A DOLLAR

It was the early fifties, busy summers in the Catskill Mountains for the resorts. Without a reservation you stood little chance of getting accommodations.

One day we received a reservation with a deposit from a single woman who requested a room with a private bath. All day long we were busy taking care of incoming guests. However, no one appeared who answered to the name of Miss Samuels. Since she made no appearance by 6 PM, we rented her room. By 10 o'clock, we were tired and relaxing in the lobby when a cabby appeared carrying two heavy valises. Following him was a willowy blond in a large straw hat. She ambled over to the desk. I got up from my seat and walked over to her. "Can I help you?"

"Why, of course. I am Miss Samuels and I have a reservation!"

I stared at her in disbelief. "Who comes at 10 o'clock? Why didn't you call to tell us you would arrive late? No one holds a room at 10 o'clock at night."

Miss Samuels looked at me nonchalantly and said, "So give me what you have available."

How do you answer? "Miss Samuels, the truth is that I have no room available."

She looked at me with eyes full of surprise. "You mean in such a large place as this you don't have even one room open?"

I looked at my bellhop who was sitting nearby. He was twirling his finger around his head to indicate that she must be daft. However, I called him over and asked, "What do we do now?" He cocked his head to one side and said, "You have an empty room on the top floor. The bed has to be put together, the room has to be cleaned up, and you have to get a chambermaid to put linen on it."

Miss Samuels was listening. "You heard what the bell-hop said. If you want to take that room we can fix it up. It has a bathroom in the hall. That's the best we can offer you for tonight!"

Miss Samuels plunked herself down in an easy chair and with her feet removed her high-heeled shoes. After a few moments she said, "The only alternative I have is to sleep in the lobby. Where can I go at this hour? I'll wait for the room that your man said was available."

Exhausted as we were, we sat around for almost an hour until the room was ready. In the meantime the bell-hop was gracious enough to go into the kitchen and heat up some coffee left in a waiter's carafe, plus some cakes from the evening meal, and bring them to Miss Samuels. She grasped the tray and started on the coffee. In the meantime, the bell-hop ran up the stairs with a chambermaid whom we had called to clean up that "reserved room with a private bath." By that time Miss Samuels was glad to have any bed to fall into, and we watched her start to climb the stairs. When she was out of sight, all of us sitting in the lobby burst out laughing. So much for the day. Wearily we struggled to our feet. Sweet dreams to Miss Samuels in her large droopy hat and her high heels. Sweet privacy, with a bath on the floor.

WHOSE CHILD IS HE?

I was standing behind the registration desk when a young man, holding a little boy by the hand, approached me. "Are your Mrs. K.?"

"Yes. What can I do for you?"

"I was told to deliver this little boy to you. You're to keep him here until further notice. Those are my instructions. Here's his valise." He turned quickly and almost ran out before I could question him.

I was greatly puzzled and walked around the counter. "What is your name, little boy?" I asked.

His lips trembled as he mumbled, "Donald. Are you my new mother?"

This was a strange situation, indeed. "Maybe," I answered.

He pulled out a slightly soiled letter and gave it to me. I read, "This is my son Donald. I don't know what to do with him. My husband and I have had a fight; he has walked out and I don't know what to do right now. I have to support myself and my parents are on vacation so I can't keep Donald with me any more. I know you are a great friend of the family and figured you could keep him until such a time as I decide if I want to keep him with me or not." A strange letter from a mother. No word of love or affection—just cold facts.

"You must be hungry Donald. Here, I'll put your valise behind my desk and you'll come with me to the children's dining room." His little body was shaking. I walked with him to the children's dining room where my two grandsons were sitting with an aunt of mine. "Aunt Annie, will you take Donald and put him next to Michael and Kenny and see that he eats. Bring him to me when they are through."

My grandsons bombarded me with questions. "Who is he and why is he here? Where are you going to put him?" "He's going to stay in your room until someone comes for him. There's no place in the hotel for a little boy alone. Please be kind to him until we find out where he belongs. You wouldn't like to be alone, would you? With you he'll have someone to talk to and won't be so scared. Come, we'll go to the house and I'll try to make him comfortable." The boys were skeptical but I had no alternative. I had a cot brought into their room and told Donald he was to sleep there. I helped him to undress. All this time Donald never uttered a word. He was a confused little boy and my heart went out to him.

"Are you my new mother? Why did my mother leave me?"

I told him "Tomorrow is another day. I'll try to find your mother or your father." I told my little two grandsons how sad it was to be left alone and that they should try to make Donald feel a little better.

After a few days the boys got into a routine, but they weren't comfortable. After all, I had imposed Donald on them. As I was walking them to their room, Kenny wanted to say something that Donald would not understand. He said, "I would like to hang a sign outside our room that says 'No Vacancy'."

Young as he was, Donald caught the drift. He cried out, "No sign. I won't go anywhere else." His tears began to flow.

"You're not going anywhere. Not until your mother or your father comes for you." That was the best I could do. I was just as troubled as the child and, besides, I was a busy woman with no time to devote to this problem. I felt that sooner or later it might resolve itself.

After a week, Donald's grandparents came to spend a few days with me. They were unaware of my situation with Donald and were shocked. When Donald saw them, his eyes lit up and he ran to them. "Grandma, grandpa, are you going to take me home?"

Grandma had married off the last of her four children and was planning a second honeymoon. Donald's abandonment interfered with her plans and she wasn't ready to give up her freedom. When she told me to keep Donald, I couldn't believe it. What kind of a grandma was she?

The next day grandma and grandpa checked out, leaving Donald behind. I could hardly focus on my work. Such selfishness! And such a bright, confused little boy. Didn't they know what they were doing to him? And to me?

About three days later, a young man came running up to my desk out of breath. "Sorry to disturb you, but is my son Donald around anywhere?" "He's having lunch with my grandsons." I replied. "Come, I'll take you there and you can have a bite with them." The joy of that reunion is still with me. It was unforgettable. The father hugged the little boy as if he would never let him go. "Don't worry, Donald, I'm taking you home. I'll never leave you again."

After a harassing meeting with both sets of grandparents, the couple decided to try again. Both felt lonely without each other and without their child. Two years later, Donald had a little sister and was on his way to becoming a normal little boy again.

His father adored him and spent a great deal of time with him, which he might not have done before.

I didn't see Donald again until twenty-five years later. I was invited to a family wedding and was introduced to Donald. What a handsome young man he had turned out to be! He was slim and had a beard. His hair was prematurely gray but most becoming. I also met his charming young wife. They were in love.

I asked his grandmother what business Donald was in. She looked at me with pride in her eyes. "Ever since Donald was a little boy he was always fascinated with airplanes and said to anyone who would listen 'I am going to be a flyer.' That was his one ambition and when he was old enough he joined the air force. He turned out to be one of the best flyers; his heart was in all aspects of flight—from the mechanics to the take off. Today he is pilot and has been promoted to captain. Now he is a happily married man. Shall I tell you a secret? Do you know how he keeps so slim? He eats raw fish."

When I questioned some of the cousins later they told me that the raw fish grandma had mentioned was called "sushi." All the male cousins got together every week and dined on sushi. They were out to preserve their figures. And they all looked beautiful.

When I was saying good-bye, Donald ran over to me and said, "I never forgot you. I'm going to give my first child your name. I love you!" That was enough for me. I went home a happy woman.

OUR CHANGING TIMES

Years ago, if you provided the daily sustenance and boasted a swimming hole or a river, you had a resort. If you had running water in the room, you really had a modern hostelry. A room with two double beds was sufficient for a family of two adults and two children—but by 1950 all that had changed.

We boasted eighty rooms with semi-private bath and shower and considered ourselves ultra modern. When a guest confided to another that she had a room with semi-private bath, she was looked upon with great respect. It cost money! By the early fifties, you only had status if you occupied one of our 'motel' styled rooms, wall to wall carpeting, colored tile bathroom, finger-tip control heating and cooling, nine-foot walk-in closets. Previously the closets were small since not too many clothes were necessary. You tried to persuade a young mother with one or two children to climb a flight of stairs. If she did, she might be 'so pooped and winded' afterwards that in desperation she would agree to a motel room.

By the '60's, a room with two beds was sufficient only for a couple and one child. When there were two children, there had to be three beds and often we had requests for four beds. If I assigned a couple to a room with one double bed, it was not unusual for the wife to say, "Ix-nay. I came for a vacation and I want two single beds." Sometimes when I assigned a couple a room with twin beds, the wife would draw me aside and whisper, "I'm here on vacation. I want to sleep with my husband if you don't mind." No wonder I'd go crazy moving beds. I've noticed, however, that it was always the wife who would ask for what she and her husband wanted. He always seemed to be the shy one. One day there will be a woman president ruling the land as she rules the pants. Years ago, when the children's mealtime bell rang, not only mamma but papa also beat a trek to the dining room with junior. If grandma was around, she came too.

About the most aggravating sight to a parent was to see another child calmly eating all the courses, while his or her angel just toyed with the food. When a child didn't eat, it cost the hotel more money because mother always ordered other dishes in the hope that one dish would appeal to her child. Then a variety of persuasions, pinchings, and story-tellings would ensue to keep junior so interested that he wouldn't be aware of how much he was eating.

I recall a mother who, determined to fatten her offspring, filled her child's glass with half sweet cream and half milk and cajoled her child until it was all gone. This was a sign for all the mammas to do the same thing. Even the fathers present were persuaded to feed this elixir. That day the balcony leading outdoors from the dining room looked like the side of a ship at sea. One child after the other was hoisted over the side to spew forth food much too rich for his or her stomach. Of course, junior had to be led back in again so that he would have some nourishment until the next meal. (Later the mothers sheepishly admitted their mistake.)

Again, late one afternoon, I walked into the kitchen to look for a snack. It had been a busy day and I had missed my lunch. Suddenly I heard a short, shrill scream and then—silence. A few moments later I heard the same shrill scream, followed by silence again. What could it be? Where did that sound come from? The third time I heard the scream, I traced it to the children's dining room. What a sight I beheld! A mother was forcing her child to lie on the table. As the child opened her mouth to scream, down went a spoonful of food. Naturally the child had to swallow it or choke. Every time she opened her mouth, down went another spoonful of food. I was shocked and angered and asked the mother whether she wanted to choke her child. She glared at me and said, "You mind your business and I'll mind mine."

I once strolled into the children's dining room and watched a mother humiliate her son so much that all the other children were staring at him. In shame he forced the food down. The mother triumphantly turned around and explained, "See, he can eat but he just wants to torture me. He ate every bit of food on his plate." I glanced at junior and he looked about ready to burst—which he did, all over the floor.

More recently (late '60's, early '70's), before a family checked in, mother wanted to know if there were counselors to supervise her child's feeding. She didn't want to be bothered getting up early, nor disturbed when playing mah jong at lunchtime. I heard one mother confiding to another, "If he doesn't want to eat, I don't want to know about it. When he's good and hungry he'll eat." Most of the time that's what happened.

Another question I was asked was, "Does your day camp take care of my children all day? I don't mean part of the day—all day! I don't want to see my children at all."

And that's exactly what we did. Our day camp was geared to take are of children all day long. After sundown, I heard "I hope your night patrol is on the job. We're clocking your girls to be sure they're making the rounds often enough. Fifteen-minute intervals are too long. We don't intend to run back and forth from the playhouse to check." (The men often listened to their wives' demands silently, but seemed to know how unfair such demands were. There was an extra tip from them at departure time.)

I recall a time when mommy or daddy or both, took care of their children. They played ball, took a son swimming, pushed a daughter on the swings, and in general amused their children. It was a happy family time. In the evening, they took turns checking on the child. The only aid we offered was a counselor (called a governess) to take care of the children during their parents' mealtime.

With changing times and demand for service, our night patrol was responsible for taking the children to the bathroom; putting them back to bed; soothing the cranky; drying the tears; covering the cold and waiting patiently for a parent to respond to an emergency.

I was happy in the thought that we had our day camp under control. We had a lovely new nursery for those children less than three years of age, staffed by several nursemaids, and a modern building with a tremendous enclosed playground for those children from three to nine years old. For the teenagers, there was a clubroom under very competent supervision. I had many compliments from parents. You can imagine my utter surprise one day when a delegation of mothers approached me and said they weren't happy with our set-up. "What more can you ask for?" I queried.

"Well," said one mother "We feel it disturbs our afternoon plans when we have to bring towels down to the pool for a dry change after their swim. Where I stayed last year, the counselors dried my children. Why don't your girls do the same?" The other mothers hung back a little sheepishly. Maybe their ringleader would succeed in making the demand for them.

My hackles rose and my thoughts weren't fit to print, but an inner voice counseled, "Hold on, but, don't let this throw you. There's no end to what people will demand of you. If you let it get you, it will." So I said as calmly as I could, "I have very nice accommodations for private maids if you wish to make such arrangements. I'll make my rates as reasonable as possible." No one was interested.

Time also was when mother would bend over the washtub in the laundry and rub away at the clothes and not mind it at all. As long as she didn't have to shop and cook and clean and wash dishes, she was satisfied to enjoy her vacation. I thought I had a modern laundry when I installed two automatic washing machines in a new laundry room that I had built but progress changed that. "What no dryers? I never heard of such a thing! I'm here on vacation!"

P.S. We now have two dryers.

Years ago, when the young folks got together evenings, they managed to have a good time by themselves. One could sing, one could play a musical instrument, one told jokes until they burst their sides laughing; there were mock marriages and hayrides. The thrill of the week was a show and dancing on the weekends by a group of ferryboat musicians. Remember them? How they scratched away so gracefully? Today, both mommy and daddy go to the playhouse (now called a night club.) dance to their hearts' content and then settle back in their seats for the show. Their very attitude says, "We're here to be entertained. Your show better be good—or else." They get a good show, too. In the end, we had to employ a master of ceremonies to select and conduct the program. We also had to do away with the 'ferryboat musicians' and employ a union band.

But we had been enjoying a false sense of security. We soon had to have a large, modern nightclub; an attractive cocktail lounge for cocktails; a modern soda fountain and snack bar. What else could anyone wish for? In this step up age, who was interested in going to bed at 12 or 1 o'clock? Life was just beginning. After the show a small group usually remained to dance, but a great many other guests got into their cars and were off to other nightclubs where they could drink and see another show. All the very big hotels now had their night clubs and special rumba bands, and our guests were beginning to ask us, "When?"

Finally we had a most colorful and outstanding nightclub with two special stage curtains (for effect). It was one of the prettiest nightclubs in the area. We even went a step ahead. We built a most attractive beauty salon with all the latest equipment. Our operators now featured a hair styling show every week. It was both an interesting and highly successful operation.

The vacation business had become a very complicated affair. There was nothing rustic about it except the grass and the trees. It was several businesses wrapped up in one. It was a restaurant; a day camp; a dance school (oh yes, we gave dance lessons every morning); a physical fitness program; a luncheonette; a theatre; a nightclub. It was an athletic campus with a baseball diamond; swimming in a gorgeous 100-foot outdoor pool; tennis courts; ping-pong, handball, badminton; volleyball. Woe betide you if you failed in any department. You'd hear about it soon enough!

And soon we once again fell by the wayside. "What! No indoor pool?"

Our hearts quivered when we heard talk elsewhere about an indoor swimming pool. If just one hotel built one, we other poor and overstressed hotelkeepers knew where our next troubles were coming from.

Our troubles really began. Now we had to look to our creditors for the money to build a pool. It was a never-ending spiral. When would it stop? When we all went broke! And so we built an indoor pool. The payoff always came when you heard mommy and daddy say, "Gee, I could use a vacation! I really need a rest."

DENTURES DO TALK

A chambermaid brought me a small box she found in one of her rooms. She couldn't remember which one. I opened the box and found an upper denture and a lower. I put the box in a cubbyhole in my desk and waited for the owner to appear. No one inquired.

At the end of the summer, I wondered what to do about the dentures. I decided to throw them into the wastebasket. But all during that day and the next, that little box seemed to say to me, "Don't throw me away. Don't throw me away." I listened and placed the box back in my drawer. Shortly after the hotel was closed for the season, my little box still rested comfortably where I had put it.

I was in the city for about two months when I received a telephone call. The man on the other end said, "You will please excuse me. I am calling for a friend. He wants to know whether anyone found a set of dentures. He is too embarrassed to call and asked me to call for him since he didn't want you to know who he was."

I said to myself, "What a nut! Why was he embarrassed? So many people wear dentures these days. Besides, dentures are an expensive affair." I told the man that I had thrown them away and then decided to recover them. However the box was in my desk drawer and, when I next made a trip to the hotel, I would bring them back.

In due time I accomplished my mission and brought the box back. I then called my inquirer and he came to pick up that little box. So you see, that little box really spoke to my mind, and I listened!

OUR CHARLIE: A MEDITATION ON THE DEATH OF A CARETAKER

He was a Polish immigrant, short in education but long in sinew. He generally got jobs hauling heavy loads. One day he was hauling furniture to my hotel in the Catskills. This country was more like home: fresh air, trees, plenty of grass and no crows. After he delivered his furniture, I was signing the slip when Charlie, the Polish man, said "Nice country, like home. Like very much." I looked at him and saw a man with a rough, kindly face. I asked him, "Would you like to work here?" The Pole's eyes shone. "Honest? You like me work for you? I'm good man—work plenty hard, no steal—honest man."

I smiled and said, "Can you come next week? I'll give you an apartment in a cottage; wood stove in the winter time; plenty of wood and coal. Not many people around but you will be comfortable. Plus a salary, of course." This sounded like heaven to Charlie and he said, "I come next week, finish my job. Like old country. Me very happy work for you."

Next week Charlie presented himself with his few belongings and was taken to the cottage he was to occupy. It had a large kitchen, nicely equipped. I said, "Today I'll take you shopping for what you need. Next week I go to the city for the winter but I'll show you around and tell you what your duties are. You will be a watchman now and look around and make repairs wherever you see the need. You will find lots of tools in the bedroom, and I'll try to give you whatever lumber and other things you need so you can keep yourself busy. I like you, Charlie, and I feel you're the man for me. I'll stay here with you this week and will come out every few weeks to see how you're doing and what you've accomplished."

"O.K. boss, I do good job, don't worry. You take me shopping and I buy plenty. I no poor man. I have some money. I'm good man; I like this country."

And that is how Charlie became our watchman and general worker at the hotel for the summer season. He had only one fault. He never waited for the waiters and bus boys to finish their tasks in the kitchen. He was impatient to wash the kitchen floor, which was a large area. Before the boys were finished, he started splashing the soapy water around them and on them in spite of their protests. He seemed to get pleasure out of making them howl and jump. I concluded he had to get his satisfactions somewhere.

When we, the family, stayed at the hotel for the summer, we became better acquainted with Charlie. During the summer he had plenty of food, the chicken and beef that guests ordered as extra courses and couldn't eat. Charlie feasted.

At the end of one summer, Charlie asked us to buy him some pigs in the spring. He said there was enough food left over from the dining room to feed at least three pigs. The hotel accommodated over four hundred people, so food for these pigs was no problem.

Came the springtime, we got Charlie three lovely black piglets. He had already built a pigpen for them. At the beginning, he got the garbage man to bring him food from other hotels that opened earlier, until he was able to feed his piglets from our own 'patch.'

Charlie and his pigs became a family. He got a great kick out of seeing his pigs, Elizabeth, John, and Mary, recognize and come running to him. And so the summer went by. When life became a little too dull, Charlie found himself at the town bar. He enjoyed his booze and when the waitresses saw his little bundle of bills, they flattered him, sat on his lap, and entertained him until he had no more bills to stuff in the Vs of their bosoms. Then he staggered happily home.

I became friendly with Charlie and was well aware of where his money went. So one day I suggested to Charlie that he give me part of his salary to save for him so he would have funds for an emergency. Charlie thought it was a good idea. He arranged to give me a portion of his salary every payday and I gave him a receipt for the amount. When he went carousing, he withdrew enough to keep him happy for the evening.

During the summer, Charlie's pigs began to show healthy signs. All the food agreed with them and their black coats became shiny. They really looked attractive and played with each other in their pen, a brick wall that encircled them so they had plenty of room to grunt and wallow. At the end of the season, Charlie had three fat sleek pigs, but their food had given out. All we had left was a couple of bags of matzo farfel from the Passover holiday. Charlie dumped the farfel in their troughs. And suddenly there was snow in the air. The pigs were insulted at such fare after what they had enjoyed during the summer.

They refused to eat. So Charlie decided it was time to dispose of them.

A few days later I walked into Charlie kitchen to see how he was faring with his pigs. I was shocked to see him with his head on the table, sobbing!

"Charlie," I shook his shoulder, "what happened?" He looked up at me with tears streaming down his face and said, "They trusted me. Elizabeth, John and Mary, and what I do? I stick knife on each heart. They're my friends, they trust me, and I kill them. I never eat them."

That shook me up. Here was an uneducated man who seemed to have more sympathy than educated people. Charlie understood his emotions better than a lot of us. Age and education have little to do with a person's attachment to animals.

True to his declaration, Charlie sadly gave his pigs away. He said that he could never eat Elizabeth, John and Mary. They were pigs, yes, but also his friends.

Charlie stayed with us for twenty-seven years. By then he was a member of the family. In the last year of his life, he had begun to ail. He suffered severe pain and when we took him to the hospital, the diagnosis was cirrhosis of the liver. Charlie was a loner and would not hear of staying in a hospital or having a nurse handle him, so we took him back to the hotel and hired another caretaker, Tom, who would also take care of Charlie as best he could. Charlie liked him and let him minister to his needs. One day, however, Charlie knew he needed the hospital. He put on his best suit and asked to be taken to his doctor. We were waiting in the car for him when Tom came running out crying, "I found him on the floor. Charlie is dead."

We advertised in the local paper that Charlie's body was lying in the funeral parlor but not one of the people to whom

Charlie had given his money appeared. Only the local plumber and his wife knelt silently at his coffin and said a prayer for him. Now Tom was in charge. He was a good, honest worker but had one problem. Every week I had to buy a gallon of wine for him. I also kept him in aspirins. I warned him that it was dangerous to mix wine with aspirin but he only laughed and said that the only way he could work and feel good was with this combination. One day Tom approached me and said he had decided to leave. The following morning he knocked at my door. He was perspiring profusely and said he wasn't feeling well and had decided to go to the hospital. He said he was a veteran and would have no trouble gaining admission.

The next morning Tom did not show up and no one went to look for him. However when he didn't appear the second day, I sent the breakfast cook, Jimmy, to see if Tom wanted breakfast. Jimmy was gone for a very long time, too long. Just as I was going to investigate, Jimmy came stomping slowly back. "Well, how's Tom" I asked. Jimmy gave me a queer look and said "I couldn't wake him, so I came back." I sent the bellhop over. He came back excited and very upset. "My God, Mrs. K! Tom's dead. He's lying in a pool of blood."

I sent two men over to clean up as best they could. Fortunately, Tom had mentioned that he was a veteran. Otherwise, he would have been buried as a pauper. But what took Jimmy so long, and why had he lied? I remembered that Tom wore a ring with a small diamond in it, a good wristwatch, and kept all his money in his wallet. And he had just collected his pay. I was stunned. I knew instantly why Jimmy had taken so long. He must have ransacked the room and helped himself to Tom's possessions. I was furious and said to Jimmy, "How could you lie? How could you rob a dead man?" He just stood behind his stove and said not a word. He hung his head and turned his back, not wanting to look at his fellow workers who were staring at him.

Thus ended the life of our caretaker's caretaker. His death left not a ripple. No one to mourn him and no one to care. Only one to pick his pockets.

A WOMAN'S WAY

Mrs. Fisher had been a guest of ours for a number of years. She always took a room on the third floor, bath-on-floor, because she didn't want to share a room but could save money by taking an inferior accommodation. A few years went by. One day I walked outside and saw to my surprise that Mrs. Fisher was standing under a tree and sobbing as if her heart would break.

"Mrs. Fisher, what are you doing here sobbing? Did anyone hurt you?"

"Oh no, Mrs. K. My son just left. He dropped me like a sack of potatoes and just ran away."

"Why did your son bring you here? You usually take a hack."

"Yes, I know. This time something happened. My husband runs a fish place in the downtown market and he had an argument with his dealer. In the middle of the fight he had an attack of apoplexy and passed out. He died right on the spot. We were all very upset and found it hard to adjust. But what was I to do in the summer? I just couldn't get myself together. My son helped me. He called for me the next day and drove me up here. But I think he was heartless to drop me off and run away."

"You mustn't forget, Mrs. Fisher, that your son did a very kind thing. He left his job to take you up here and I guess he hurried away to return to his job. So you should feel grateful.

43

Come with me and I'll get someone to help you with your luggage and make you comfortable."

Mrs. Fisher spent several weeks with us and went home in a more cheerful, reconciled mood. I did not hear from her the following summer. But the season after that, I got a call from her asking me to reserve a deluxe, private room for her. She was coming out with her new husband.

A very charming couple approached me and it took a few moments for me to recognize Mrs. Fisher. No more the plain, dowdy woman who climbed to the top floor. Facing me was a glamorous woman. She had a lovely hairdo; her face looked as if it had undergone extensive cosmetic treatments. Her clothes fitted her perfectly. She wore a mink stole, which was the fashion at that time. Any woman wearing one was considered in the moneyed class. She smiled up at me and said, "I hope you have a good room for us. It must have a private bath, you know, and I don't care to climb any stairs."

I decided to show them a room myself, and took them to a private room on the main floor, no steps. Mrs. Fisher looked at me and shook her head. "This isn't what I want. I want a large, deluxe room where my husband and I can be comfortable." In Yiddish I said to her, "As you have always been accustomed to." I led them to a room that satisfied her. Her husband was a fairly tall pleasant looking man and he said to me, "Whatever pleases my wife will please me as well." The bellhop checked them in.

Where were those crocodile tears she had shed under the tree? Romance always makes a difference.

A DOG'S STORY

Rose was a retired schoolteacher, rather tall, with soft gray eyes, slightly gray hair and always a worried expression. Now she had applied for a job at the front desk as clerk. She looked honest and reliable and I gave her the job, checking in and registering the guests.

She wasn't very talkative, but after some time she joined a life-story discussion between the bookkeeper and the telephone operator. "I've had my ups and downs, maybe more than most people. I had two miscarriages before I gave birth to a live baby girl. Maybe I became overprotective. Every minor mishap became a major problem; I know I magnified each one because I am a natural worrier. Unfortunately, I instilled that same feeling in my daughter and taught her to come to me with every little complaint. Now she's always unsure. She just called me to say that she had a flat in her car and where should she go? This upsets me because it's my fault that she's so unsure of herself. She is now an adult and seeks my advice about every little thing. It's a relief to me to be here among definitive people. As you see, I haven't asked for any pay for my job. I'm satisfied to have a room with a private bath and all my meals." She looked at me and said, "I'm really happy to be near you because you never seem to be worried about any situation; you solve your problems as they come up and that gives me a lift. I try to do the same and it sure does help. I also know that I can come to you with any problem and you won't turn me down."

That's why Rose has been with me for several years, never leaving the desk for all seven days of the week and only attending one of our nightly shows or taking care of her personal needs. Every week or so she gets an excited telephone call from her daughter. "Mom, I can't decide what dress to buy or, do you think I should also buy a suit or, do you think I should go out with Dave again?"

Dorothy, Rose's daughter, cherished a dog. He was her only roommate. She spoke to him as if he understood what she was saying. She loved and adored that dog and treated him as if he were a child. If she had to take the dog out for a walk, she made sure no one was in the elevator because it might upset him. She also kept him away from people. He always stayed at her side and she babied him. She fed him by hand, talked to him, kissed him and made his bed as comfortable as possible. The dog knew no other life.

One week, Dorothy came to visit her mother. When the lobby was clear, she hurried the dog into the office where her mother was. The dog huddled beside Rose. When Dorothy went into the dining room with her mother, they tied the dog to a chair in the back office. Several times during the meal Dorothy ran out to check her baby.

The time came when Dorothy met an attractive young man and they began to date. Soon they were talking about an engagement. Dorothy called her mother and Rose met him over one weekend. Rose gave her approval and in due time they were married. Rose was happy. Now her daughter wouldn't lean on her so often.

The following summer, Rose got an excited call from her daughter. She was pregnant and Rose was ecstatic. She spent a lot of time worrying, however, since she remembered her own problem. Soon she was grandmother to a bouncing baby boy.

Now Dorothy had a problem. She did not want her dog around her baby. She always feared for the child's safety and finally called her mother again.

"Mother, I don't want the dog in my house. I'm calling to ask you to take him to the hotel where he could stay with you. You are the only one who can handle him."

Rose was shocked. She wasn't happy about taking the dog but was worried whether she would be allowed to keep him in her room. It never crossed her mind to refuse and finally the dog became her charge. She had one problem. The dog hid under her bed and refused to come out. Rose had to move her bed and carry the dog. As soon as the dog had done his duty he slid under the bed again until Rose shoved his food to him.

One day Rose decided to take the dog to the office. She worried too much about his being locked in all day, every day. Soon the dog became accustomed to sleeping under her chair. When Rose decided to take him out, she would wait until the lobby was clear so the dog wouldn't tremble when he was walked.

Toward the end of the summer, Dorothy visited with her husband and the baby. She had a room in a bungalow near the main house. The dog barked happily when he recognized his 'mother' but Dorothy paid him no attention. She ignored him completely. At night, it was suddenly a different situation. The dog refused to go with Rose to her room. When Rose held the leash loosely, the dog slipped away from her and ran to the bungalow where Dorothy slept. He pawed at the door and let out small moans, but Dorothy was adamant. She wanted no part of the dog. He lay in the hallway all night and couldn't be forced away. When Dorothy and her family went out to breakfast, he followed her. He was tied to Rose's chair and there he stayed all day. After lunch Dorothy and her family packed to leave. When she came to say goodbye, Rose asked her if she were taking the dog with her. Dorothy looked at her in surprise.

"I thought I told you that I wanted no part of that dog. I don't want him near my child. You can keep him here with you. If you don't want to take him home, leave him here with the owner. I'm sure he'll be well taken care of. I don't want him."

How could a woman who had been so close to an animal, feeding him, loving him, worrying about him, suddenly develop distaste for even having him near her? She said her good-byes to everyone, got into her car and left without a second glance at the dog or her distraught mother. Rose could handle everything. Didn't she always solve all her problems?

At the end of the season, Rose said in a scared voice "I don't plan to take him home with me. I have enough to take care of myself without taking care of a high strung dog. Maybe you can find someone who can love and take care of him."

And so it was that I had a dog on my hands. I didn't give him away. I had an idea and wanted to see if it could work. I chained the dog, whom I shall call Fido, to the front of my house and let him stay there for about three days so that he would be acquainted with his new home. I placed a bowl of dog food before him. The first day he just sniffed at the food, but the second day hunger overcame him and he ate. The third day he seemed restless and I unhooked the chain. For a few moments he seemed uncertain just what he could do. He took a few steps—nothing happened—so he took a few more and seeing that he had no chain, he started to walk away slowly. That felt good so he walked some more and then, suddenly, he started to run. I watched him. First he ran to the bungalow where Dorothy had stayed. The door was open and he wandered around and then walked out. He stood for a moment irresolutely and then started to run. I watched him as he ran up the steps of every bungalow, sniffing at each door. Suddenly he disappeared and I saw him no more that day.

The next morning I asked Albert, the caretaker, to find him. After a half hour Albert came back carrying Fido under his arm. He found Fido crouched under one of the bungalows. We then gave him a bowl of food and chained him up until the next day when we let him loose. Albert had to hunt for Fido again and bring him back. This happened again for the next two days. Then I decided to let Fido loose and see what happened. I didn't feel like playing this catch game any more. If Fido didn't want to come home, so be it. Enough was enough. So now Fido was on his own. He did not come home for two days. The third day, he was eating the food I had left out for him. He also let Albert come near him without flinching. He was gaining self-confidence and even looked up to me when I approached. Soon Fido was wandering away on his own, digging up some earth, investigating piles of old wood.

At that time, Mike, one of my grandsons, called and asked if I would take care of his dog. Since he had planned to be gone for about three weeks, he felt his dog would be better off with me up here instead of being boarded out. My grandson felt that the country air and the food would be better for him. Soon my grandson's dog, Bobo, was vacationing with me. At first, Fido growled a bit when Bobo approached him. Then I placed their two bowls of food near each other and they started eating together. After two days of this proximity, I unchained both dogs and suddenly they were romping together. Fido fairly flew over rocks with Bobo leading the way. They fell into muddy water and came back full of mud but whining happily. First Albert hosed them off and then they ate together. From that time on they were inseparable. They always romped together and always ate together.

Now it was the time for Mike to come up and take his beloved Bobo home with him. What was going to happen to Fido?

Mike watched them at play and looked at me. He said, "It would be a shame to separate them. Maybe I should take Fido home with me. Bobo will then have a friend to keep him company and on week-ends they would have a good time together at my cabin in the woods." And that is what happened to Fido. He was now a normal dog and was going to live a normal dog's life—maybe having a girlfriend as well. I watched Mike haul both dogs into his car and, waving goodbye, he took off with the two friends. What a relief!

ON SEEKING A
WOMAN

A hand was laid across the paper I was writing on at the front desk. I looked up to see a nattily dressed man smiling at me. He looked familiar and I knew that we had met before but I couldn't place him. He wore a navy blue suit with gold buttons, like some naval captain, with gold braid around the collar.

"Don't you recognize me, Mrs. K?" I hesitated and then said, "I'm sure we've met but I can't seem to remember your name." He laughed and said, "I'm Mr. Diamond, a former guest. My wife and I occupied room 4 in the Sinbad." My goodness, was that the former sloppy, henpecked man I remembered? His wife used to embarrass him in public with her sarcastic remarks. He bore it quietly but there was resentment in his eyes. Especially when they came to pay their bill. "Such a man! Such an old car! Look at my clothes!" I knew they could afford more but it wasn't his fault. He'd say in a meek voice "That's the way she wants it." She would then pull out her checkbook and grudgingly pay the bill.

Here was a man full of life, wearing a smart suit, especially the beret that made him look like an artist. Now I remembered Mr. Diamond. "Why are you here alone and where did you come from? You're not staying here, I'm sure. Where are you?"

He smiled at me and said, "My wife was killed crossing a street and here I am a free man. I never gave her my whole salary. I always kept a little roll for myself without her knowing or she would have taken it from me. Now I have several thousand dollars besides her bank account. So I decided to go to a hotel where I might meet a rich woman. I'm staying at the Pines and have a private room for myself. Much better that that cheesy room my wife always took."

"How much are you paying?" I asked. He looked at me a moment and said "I'm paying enough, $850 a week, but for once I am enjoying the atmosphere, the service, and plenty of ladies to keep me company." "And looking for a rich man" I said. "You are all fooling each other."

"That's why I came here. I met a nice woman and I wanted you to meet her. I wanted to get your opinion. I don't want to fall in."

"Bring her over if you like, but call me first. I'm a busy woman but am always interested in love affairs." He saluted me and said, "I'm so happy to talk to you. You have always been good to me."

The following week, there was Mr. Diamond and his 'girl-friend'. If ever I saw a 'tizzy,' she was it. Her face was painted; long earrings dangled from her ears. Her shiny red nails were as long as claws. She wore a tight fitting dress and there was a knowing smile on her face. This was the glamour girl Mr. Diamond had picked? I could understand his attraction to her. His wife had been a real Yiddish mama and dressed like one. Ordinary housedresses and a face devoid of color. This woman was the opposite, but he could not tell dross from gold. I could imagine what kind of a wife she would make. It wouldn't have taken long before his bankroll would be gone. How could I tell him? Finally I said, "Mr. Diamond, if you come into my office I will show a little box of articles we found in your room after you left. To the girlfriend I said, "If you will excuse us, it will take just a few minutes." I waved her to a chair and ushered Mr. Diamond into my office.

"Mr. Diamond, you asked me to meet your girlfriend and I am glad you did. Do you think you would be happy with her? She must think you are a wealthy man and that's what she's looking for. I doubt if she is a wealthy woman." His face fell. "I have a lot of respect for your opinion but want to think about it." About two weeks later there was a dejected man standing in front of me. I looked up and said "Well?" Tears were shining in his eyes. "I've learned my lesson. I was so crazy about her that I lent her $500. She promised me all kinds of favors. When we were in the playhouse (she didn't come with me) I saw her dancing with a much younger man. When I asked her for a dance she turned her head away and said, "I am here with a date and want to spend the evening with him." "Can you imagine my shock? What about the money she borrowed from me?" I smiled to myself and said, "Mr. Diamond, you got away cheap. You don't know how lucky you are. She might have gotten more from you but you were luckier than that. You might have married her and then what? You would have had a worse life than with your wife."

Mr. Diamond was quiet for a while and then said, "Would you mind if I left the Pines and checked in here? I don't want to be in the same place anymore." I gave him a nice, private room and he seemed to come back to life again. He was having a lovely time and I didn't see him again for more than two weeks. Then one day Mr. Diamond stood before me. He was a little shamefaced but said to me, "What do you think of Mrs. Rosen?

I feel so much at home with her. We sit at the same table and she advises me about the various dishes. She makes me put on a heavy jacket in the cold evenings and always looks to my comfort. No one else has ever worried about me like that, and the funny part is that I feel the same way about her. What do you think?"

"I think Mrs. Rosen is a lovely woman. I've known her for years. She is gentle, kind, and trustworthy. I believe you could be happy with her. Oh, and Mr. Diamond, Mrs. Rosen is a very, very wealthy woman. Good luck to you!"

THE AFFAIR

One day I got a call from Emily, the daughter of a friend of mine, a very successful business executive. She said, "Aunt Carrie, please reserve a nice private room in a quiet place for me. I am so tired and exhausted that I could sleep for weeks. I'll be out in a few days."

When Emily checked in, I didn't see her for a whole day. She slipped into the dining room for the evening meal. After dinner, from my desk, I saw her walking out with one of my guests, a tall, personable young man in his thirties, one of her table mates. The next day she came in for her lunch and dinner, again walking out with her table mate, whose name was Alex.

It seems they had found mutual interests! Soon they were playing tennis, swimming, hiking, attending the nightly shows and gliding along on the dance floor. It isn't often that young people of Emily's type find people interesting enough to hold their attention, so I was doubly happy that Emily was pleasantly occupied.

Before her two weeks were up, Emily suddenly came into my office and said, "Aunt Carrie, I'm leaving in the morning." This was so sudden that I was taken aback. "What happened?" I asked. Her eyes flashed for a moment and then she said, "He wanted to have an affair!"

"How wonderful!" I cried. "I'll make an affair that you will never forget—the best food, the best music, the best of everything!"

Emily just stared at me. "Come off it, Aunt Carrie! I thought you were an experienced hotelkeeper. He wasn't talking about food. He was talking about sex. Sex! Get it? My mind was so full of romance that I thought—love."

The next afternoon, after lunch, an excited and disturbed young man began stuttering, "What happened to Emily? Where did she go?"

"You should know better than to ask me. I believe you made an improper proposal to her and she ran."

"I must have been out of my mind. I was so crazy about her that I just wanted to love her. I meant no harm. What do I do now? I don't want to lose her. Can you give me a number where I can reach her?"

"I would be abusing her confidence if I did that. I'll tell you what. I'll call her at home this evening and ask her. I'll do the best I can."

"Tell her that if she wants an affair, I'm willing to wait until she's ready—maybe next spring—and she can have the affair here at the hotel."

It's true that I jumped to the wrong conclusion the first time, but I was more than certain it was going to be the right one this time.

THE PRINCESS

At the age of ten, little Harry was not allowed to play with his friends after school. There was so much work to be done on the farm that he had to help. He had two sisters. Mrs. Fried always sighed, "Why couldn't I have had three boys? It would have been so much easier."

The cows' stalls had to be cleaned out. Harry pushed out as much of the dung as he could with a shovel. His favorite job was the chicken coop. He loved to feel around in the nests and take out the warm eggs. His delight was breakfast: scrambled, fried, boiled or any which way. With his mother's delicious home-baked bread and butter mingled with the taste of the rich milk he squeezed from a cow, he went to school with a satisfied belly.

One day when Harry was helping, he saw flames shooting from the barn. He was petrified. Soon the fire engines were spraying the barn, but it had burned so fast that only charred pieces of wood remained.

Since I was a neighbor, I got into my car and visited the scene of destruction. Harry was standing in the debris, looking helpless. I went over to him. "I'm sorry about the fire. Your parents must be very upset."

"Yes, they are," Harry replied.

I guessed, "Too bad they didn't have time to take out the cows."

Harry looked up at me in surprise. "Of course they did. All the cows are in back of the field behind our house."

I thought it was fortunate for the parents that I was not the insurance adjuster.

In his high school days, Harry's duties were a little different. The family occupied a big, rambling steam-heated building inherited from a previous generation. There were lots of unused rooms, formerly lived in by several families at a time.

Now the Frieds had different ideas. It was tough work managing a farm. Mrs. Fried had been toying with the idea of running a boarding house and this was her chance. She hired a Polish woman to help clean up the vacant rooms. The furniture was there and the two women worked hard to make the house attractive. Mrs. Fried frequented second hand stores in the area and bought hotel china and silver, kitchen equipment, and whatever she felt would be needed. Finally, Mrs. Fried happily put out her shingle, "Rooms for Rent." Woodbourne was a small hamlet but boasted a 'first offense prison,' and there were many demands from visitors to the prison as well as workers employed there.

Now Harry spent a good part of the day at school, but the china and silver were left for him to clean when he came home—a duty he hated. However, the little hotel prospered. There was only one waiter, but serving in those days was easier. At breakfast time he went around with three baskets of soft, medium and hard eggs. Bread, butter, and milk were on the table. There were long benches instead of chairs at the tables; meals were served family style—just two choices—and dessert: home-baked coffeecake and whatever Mrs. Fried's repertoire consisted of. When the Polish woman's work was finished in the kitchen, she became the chambermaid.

Mr. Fried did all the shopping. A whole calf was $6.00; a full cow $10.00. Rates for room and board were $15.00 a week for a room with a connecting bath; $12.50 for room with bath nearby. Business was progressing. The town of Woodbourne soon acquired a post office, a grocery combined with a bakery, and a liquor store.

When it was time for college, Harry had his mind made up to become a teacher and studied to achieve that goal. In his last year, he became conscious of an attractive female classmate. She was smartly dressed, had a lovely figure, and was quite appealing. While most of the young men paid homage to Sally, Harry had no time for diversion. He had to get home as quickly as he could to take care of his job. His parents needed him. Now Harry was a fairly good-looking, tall young man with an earnest, pleasant face. His body was quite muscular from his farm days. But he was shy where girls were concerned, and remained closely attentive to his studies.

Sally was piqued that Harry never paid attention to her. She was also attracted to him and was trying to figure out a way to engage him, which was difficult because he was out of the room as soon as class was over. On his way home, Harry's thoughts were of Sally, Sally, and Sally.

One day, in his hurry to get out of the classroom, Harry tripped over the leg of a desk. Sally rushed to his aid but Harry had already picked himself up. "Are you hurt? Can I help you?"

"Thank you. I believe I'm O.K."

Sally was not going to give up so easily. She walked Harry to the door and said, "I'm having a little party at my house this Saturday night. I would love to have you be one of my guests."

Harry looked into her eyes and saw she was pleading. His heart was filled with a stabbing pain of joy. For a moment he was speechless and then muttered, "I have to run now but if you'll give me your address in class tomorrow, I'll really try to come." This gave Sally time to arrange the party, which had just been born in her mind. She wasn't going to let Harry get away.

Saturday evening came and Harry was so nervous about what to wear that he was almost in a state of collapse. However, the party was a lovely affair. Just a handful of Sally's friends and her parents attended. They served appetizing delicacies. Harry felt at ease and, quite surprisingly, very much at home. When the party was over, Sally held on to Harry's arm and said, "Don't leave yet. Let's sit outside on the porch swing for a while. I'd like to talk with you." How could Harry refuse? His heart gave a strong leap. How did she know that was just what he wanted? He felt he could stay with her forever.

They sat close together and the impact of her body close to his was frightening to him. Desires he had not known existed rendered him speechless. What he did not know was that Sally was experiencing similar feeling. Both were silent for quite a while. Sally took the initiative. She faced him, touched his face with her hands and said, "It feels wonderful just to sit here with you, Harry. Do you feel the same?" She pressed her face close to his and before he was aware of what he was doing, he was kissing her passionately. Sally happily responded.

When he was able to control himself, Harry whispered, "What am I doing? Please forgive me. It was so sudden."

Sally answered, "What is there to forgive? It was wonderful, Harry. Let's become good friends."

"I wish we could. It's so difficult for me to get away—with all the work I have to do before I can even study."

"You must find a way. Life is not all work. Insist on having more help. You're entitled to some freedom and I'd like to be with you whenever possible."

After much hassling at home, Harry and Sally managed to spend time together. They found endless topics to discuss and much time for loving. This was Harry's first love affair and he felt that all he wanted was just Sally. There was no doubt in Sally's mind, either. She was eager to belong to him.

At graduation time, it was definite. Sally and Harry were to be married and her parents were happy to arrange the wedding. They liked the young man Sally was in love with. They found him serious, hard working, honest and devoted to their daughter.

Soon Harry was teaching. He loved his work. He was assigned to young teenagers, teaching and coaching. His specialty was composition; he assigned papers discussing ideas on home life, friendship, jobs or professions. This was Harry's pet subject, springing from his own youth and ambitions. The students were as engaged by these topics as Harry was. The students explored their thoughts by writing about the frustration of children living in a small town.

As for Sally, she was happy as a receptionist at a large insurance house in Monticello. Here she could wear all her lovely clothes and meet all types of people, sometimes even making a friend. Newspapers were always on the tables in the waiting room. Whenever Sally had a chance, she scanned the headlines and read the gossip. This prince or princess, that business tycoon, this wealthy dowager was giving a party. An idea simmered in Sally's mind. Why was she so different from these people? It would be fun to be treated as royalty, to have every wish granted by a nod or a shake of her head. She had the jewelry her mother had presented to her on her wedding day. A necklace with a magnificent square emerald surrounded by diamonds in a heart shape; a pair of matching earrings with an emerald surrounded by diamonds from her aunt (her mother's sister), inherited from a great grandmother years ago. Sally liked to envision that they originally came from a pirate ship. With these jewels and her clothes, she could look like a princess. The idea haunted Sally and one evening she said to Harry, "Would you object if I took Christmas week off to go to New York City to do some shopping, and then maybe even go to Radio City? I would love it and you could take that rest you need so much. You can sleep late, eat when you want, dress when you want. Lately you've seemed so tired you've actually been falling into bed. What do you think?"

"If you want to know, I've been thinking of two things. I'd like to spend the holiday with you, but the idea of a complete rest appeals to me too."

"Let me make up your mind for you. You take that rest and before you know it, I'll be home again."

And that is how Sally got to make her reservation at the Carlyle Hotel in New York. Wasn't that where royalty always went? Well, that was where Sally was going to go. Money was no object. Sally's parents had given her a substantial dowry (she was the only child). Sally meant to pursue her dominating ambition.

Her reservation was made well in advance of the holiday. Sally started making preparations: new dresses and an evening gown, a red cashmere cape with shoes to match. Since Sally planned to take her pet poodle with her, she had jackets made for her pet to match each dress. When the holiday rolled around, Sally was ready. Harry unhappily escorted her to the depot where a bus would take her to the Port Authority in New York. He regretted letting her talk him into this trip, but he also looked forward to spending a sloppy week, waking, eating, and sleeping as the mood hit him. Oh well, he couldn't have his cake and eat it too. As Sally said, in a week she would be back home.

At the Port Authority, Sally hailed a cab to the Carlyle. She was on her way. At the Carlyle, a liveried doorman helped her out of the cab with her luggage, but Sally kept her poodle on his leash. He wore a jacket that matched the color of her cape. She made a striking entrance. The bellhop carried her luggage to the registration desk. Sally registered as "Princess Sally." The clerk raised her eyebrows, but ordered the bellhop to take her to her room. There, he put her suitcases down and wished her a happy holiday. Sally tipped him and he thanked her effusively—the tip had satisfied him. She then sank down into an easy chair, but before she could relax, there was a knock on the door. A maid appeared. "I come to help you unpack, Madame." With Sally's permission, she proceeded to open the valises, hang up the dresses, put away the underwear and the shoes, and prepare a bath. She even put all the contents of Sally's make-up kit in their proper places on a dressing table.

Such service! Sally had nothing to do but enjoy it. She tipped the maid and finally began to relax. She fell asleep in her chair. When she awoke it was close to dinnertime. Before taking her bath, she called for a dinner reservation. Wasn't it wonderful? All you had to do was to walk into the dining room and, presto, you could have whatever you wanted to eat. The waiter brought her a menu, disappeared briefly, and then came back to take her order. Sally was momentarily confused and asked, "What would you suggest?" The waiter pointed to an item and said, "This is the specialty of the day and you will really enjoy it." Sally ordered it, enjoyed it, and was pleased with herself. There was a little note on the table inviting the diners to a special show in the nightclub at nine p.m.

This was an unexpected joy to Sally. She had been wondering whether she would have to take her wedding gown home untouched. She dressed with unusual care. Her white satin wedding gown, her green shoes to match her emeralds, a green silk scarf, and a tiara of rhinestones on her lovely auburn hair. She was pleased with what she saw in the mirror, but was she overdressed? Too late. She went down to the nightclub and hesitated in the doorway. She was wondering which way to go when the band, or rather the drums, beat a loud tattoo. Suddenly a spotlight revealed Sally standing by the entrance. She made an unusually charming figure. All eyes turned to this apparition, who looked like a royal princess with her childlike expression and a vulnerability so striking that many women felt close to tears at this reminder of their childhood fantasies.

Before Sally could move, a pair of hands seized hers and drew her to the dance floor. The band had begun to play an elegant fox trot. She had to follow her partner's footsteps. He was guiding her along expertly and Sally soon fell in step with him. She felt his eyes on her as they were whenever she stole a glance at him. To her he seemed middle-aged, though he was really thirty-five years old (as she later found out). He told her his name was Paul and she told him that she was Princess Sally.

After the dance, he guided her to his table and said "Won't you please join us. These are my friends." He introduced her to the couple seated at the table. "Count and Mrs. Seagram, this is Princess Sally." She responded with a smile, beginning to feel more comfortable. When she ordered an orange soda on the rocks, her partner ordered the same, saying, "If it's good for you, it's good for me." He kept stealing glances at her when he thought she wasn't looking, but Sally was quite aware of his scrutiny.

When the band struck up again, the Count rose and approached Sally. Paul rose hastily and led her onto the dance floor. He smiled down at her and said, "One dance is not enough for me. I feel as if I could go on for the rest of the night." Sally was a little taken aback but said, "You're a man of admirable ambition." Before she could finish her thoughts he clasped a soft hand over her mouth and said, "No comment. That's how I feel." They finished the dance in silent harmony and returned to their seats.

The lights dimmed and the show began, much to Sally's relief. Her partner seemed mesmerized. He continuously studied her. Sally pretended not to notice. The show featured a famous comedian and the audience was delighted with him. When the act concluded after many encores, the lights came on and Sally rose, saying to her tablemates, "Thank you for making my evening so pleasant. I must rest now." As she got up to leave, Paul also rose and said, "I'll accompany you." He held her by the elbow and escorted her to the lobby. He wasn't going to give up so easily. "How about coming up to the roof garden for a bit of fresh air?" Sally hesitated and then said, "I'm not dressed for the outdoors."

"You can take my jacket, or we can go to your room for your wrap."

"I'd rather wear something of my own." They went to her room and he waited outside. Sally emerged with a glowing red cape. He was stunned.

They strolled to the roof garden. Paul said, "I know you must think I'm daffy, but I must confide to you that in the past ten years I have never felt any desire to look at or talk to a woman. The day I was to have married, my bride was in a fatal accident and I went to a funeral instead of a wedding. I'm astonished at myself. I don't know how I reached your side or asked you to dance with me. It seemed as natural as breathing."

Poor Sally. She wanted to be a princess just for a week. She liked this young man, but she was a married woman and loved Harry dearly. She wished this was not happening and that she was safely home.

She wakened a bit late the next morning. When she walked out of the lobby, she found Paul standing and talking to the doorman. She said good morning as she passed them, but found Paul keeping in step with her.

"I'm going for my breakfast," she said.

"I'd like to join you if I may." He kept walking until Sally reached the little coffee shop where she planned to breakfast. They both ate together and Sally said, "It was nice of you to breakfast with me, but now I'm going to take a walk with my little dog."

"Just a minute, please. I have the morning free. I don't have a business appointment until 4 o'clock this afternoon. I'd love to spend the morning with you."

Poor Sally. How could she be rude and tell him to go? In two days she would be safely home. They strolled into Central Park and sat under a shaded tree where Sally wanted to rest. They sat quietly for a while and then Sally decided to talk. "When I told you last night at the table that I inhabited a little island off the sea where I sat on a throne and ruled, meting out justice and ordering the strongest men to pan for gold so that when my coffers were full I could purchase the adjoining island, I was, as you know, having a good time. Now I'll give you the true picture. I am just an ordinary Jewish girl from the Catskills with a lot of fancy dreams. The Carlyle was one of them. For a week I was a princess. Now the dream is over and I go back to my little island which is a small hamlet in the Catskill Mountains."

Paul studied her a moment, then he said, "To me you will always be a princess. Thank you for telling me what I already knew. It doesn't change my feeling for you. I adore you, but that circlet on your left finger has disturbed me. I wish it wasn't there. I wish you were mine. I could think of no greater happiness than to cherish you for the rest of my life. I know this might sound a little crazy, but my heart led me to you before I had even spoken a word to you and I still feel the same. I'd like to have dinner with you once more this evening. In the morning I fly back to England, where I have my home. Here is my card. If you should ever be in need, please remember that I will always be here for you." Paul bent over and kissed Sally. There were tears in her eyes and Paul kissed them away. "See you tonight, Princess." Sally watched him walk away.

She was in such a confused state that she didn't know whether to laugh or cry. Why did this happen to her? It certainly wasn't in her plan. She was surprised at how much pain she felt.

Sally found herself looking forward to that dinner. She hadn't wanted to part in the park, but she also didn't want to suffer her mixed feelings.

She found Paul waiting for her and together they ordered dinner. They both felt sad, but Sally rose to the occasion. "You know, Paul, you never told me much about yourself. It would be interesting to me to know a few of the highlights in your life."

Paul seemed to find relief in talking to her about some of the high and not so high points in his life. It brought him closer to her and before they both knew it, dinner was over. Paul escorted her once more to the roof deck.

They had stood for a while leaning against the railing when Paul took her in his arms and kissed her as if he would never stop. It was to last a lifetime. When his tongue sought hers, Sally pulled herself away and ran down to her room.

And so the week ended for the princess. Arriving home, she raced from the bus and literally fell into Harry's arms. She hadn't realized how much she had missed him. She buried her head in his shoulder and clung to him. "Oh Harry, just keep kissing me. I feel so safe with you."

Sally walked into the dining room and found the table set with candles, a bowl of fresh cut flowers in the center and a parcel in front of her seat. She burst into tears. "Oh Harry, it's so good to be back home again and live normally. Merry, merry Christmas. You know I'm not really your princess. I am really your queen."

STALKING A HUSBAND

Mrs. Meyer, a widow, arrived at the Aladdin with a purpose. She had made up her mind to alter her situation and what better place to meet a man than a hotel? She came fully determined and prepared. She sat on a sofa in the lobby facing the registration desk so she could observe the incoming guests. Whenever a single man appeared, she was right at his elbow. "My name is Hilda Meyers and since you are alone, would you mind sitting at my table? It would be nice to have some good company to enjoy with meals." If she was snubbed it made no difference. Her motto was "If you don't succeed, try and try again."

I became irritated at her persistence but she was not deterred. She had no intention of relinquishing her purpose. This is what she came for and what she was using her hard-earned money to accomplish.

After two days, a little Jewish man appeared pleased at Mrs. Meyers's attention. He seemed to be happy that someone wanted his company and readily agreed to join her. They seemed to hit it off very quickly—he was a lonely man and she was a determined woman. They spent two weeks enjoying each other at the table and then spending the afternoons separately. But in the evenings they were always together at a reserved table, watching the shows and then dancing afterwards.

I had no time to watch the entertainment, but I asked our master of ceremonies to observe these two and tell me what was happening. After one show, my emcee came to visit me in the lobby. He said, "I have never seen such an enraptured man as Mr. Levy. He doesn't take his eyes off his lady-friend, and they don't seem to be aware of the people around them. He puts his face close to hers; she holds him tighter. When the dance is over, they stand in a corner holding hands until the next dance. When they go out they have their arms around each other, unaware of people watching them. But why are you interested?"

I explained the situation to him and he laughed. "It looks like the lady is succeeding. Good luck to her!"

At the end of two weeks, Mr. Levy came over to pay his bill. He had a sheepish look on his face and said, "Will you please have Mrs. Meyers's bill ready also. We plan to leave together and maybe, maybe." He left the rest up in the air.

Towards the end of the summer, one of the guests approached the desk and said, "Would you believe it? Mrs. Meyers and Mr. Levy are getting married. I hear that they are planning a Florida honeymoon. She got her man and she also seems to be happy with him."

The following summer, at the beginning of July, I noticed two women walking through the lobby. On further inspection, I recognized Mrs. Meyers. She was an entirely different woman. She was wearing beautiful clothes and had on some lovely jewelry, including a large diamond ring. She looked like a glamorous, well-fed woman. Her friend was holding her arm and they seemed deep in conversation.

I asked Mrs. Meyers whether she was planning to spend her vacation with us this year. She looked disdainfully at me and said, "I was only showing my friend where I spent my vacation last year. I wouldn't think of coming back here. I'm stopping at a classy hotel. I have a room with private bath for myself and can afford to stay for the summer. I pay five hundred dollars a week. My husband died suddenly. Maybe I'll meet someone where I am staying."

A FREE HUSBAND

They were a middle-aged couple, Dr. and Mrs. Morrow, and occupied a bungalow which they had been renting from me for many years. They had made a number of friends and the Aladdin had become a summer home for them. They did some walking, some physical training exercises, and attended the hotel shows every evening. Dr. Morrow, a retired dentist, was a quiet, self-contained man; his wife Lorraine was more talkative and made friends easily.

The summer Mrs. Morrow started ailing, she kept Dr. Morrow by her side. He waited on her hand and foot. He complained to the management if the heater in their room wasn't warm enough; if the TV wasn't clear enough; if the maid didn't come in early enough; if the people were talking too loudly near the bungalow. In fact, Mrs. Morrow must have complained about everything she could think of to keep Dr. Morrow hopping. He didn't seem to mind if it placated her.

The following summer when the Morrows arrived, Mrs. Morrow looked thinner and quite ill. However, she said she wanted to come back because she was lonely at home and she believed the mountain air would help her. As usual, Dr. Morrow was her errand boy. At least there was someone she could order about and who obeyed uncomplainingly. He must have known how ill she really was.

One day, as I was standing at my desk, I looked up and saw Mrs. Morrow struggling to go up the four steps into the lobby. I ran to her and helped her into a comfortable chair. "Why did you come? It's such an effort for you."

She looked up at me and said, "I just wanted to join the human race for a change. I wanted to have some people around me." She sat there and many guests stopped and chatted with her. She gradually relaxed and even had a smile on her face. And so the summer ended.

The following summer, Dr. Morrow came alone. We all extended our sympathy. He said he knew of no other summer home and was happy to be among friends again. The next day, there was Dr. Morrow with the dance class, seeming to enjoy himself. A day or two later when I passed the dance class, Dr. Morrow looked up. When he saw me he ran over and kissed me. He looked such a happy man that I was amazed. Not only did he take dance lessons, he joined the swim club and looked athletic in a new swimsuit. And that wasn't all. In the evening, he was dancing with the ladies.

One day an attractive single woman checked in. The first thing she said to me was, "I'm available." Just like that. She was on the hunt. It wasn't long before she attached herself to Dr. Morrow. He wasn't quite ready. He wanted to be free to explore the field and enjoy the attention he was receiving from the female guests. He was a marvel to behold. He looked ten years younger, running to quickly greet a newcomer. He smiled to everyone, ran up and down the lobby steps, opened the entrance door for anyone coming in, and presenting with a courtly bow. The moth had become a butterfly.

In due time, the 'available woman' had her clutches on Dr. Morrow. And when a determined woman makes up her mind, she doesn't loosen her tentacles. Soon they were always seen together. Dr. Morrow sported a little mustache and he became the romeo of the hotel.

Toward the end of the season, Dr. Morrow came up to me and said, "I have to ask your advice. My girlfriend wants me to be her steady. She even promises to buy a home in Lake Louise so that we can be near the hotel to see the shows, to dance, to have dinner here, and so on. What do you think?" I looked at him thoughtfully and asked him to make sure he wasn't making a mistake. To be sure that they would be compatible, I made a suggestion. "You aren't a baby anymore. Why don't you live together until you're sure she is the one for you?" He looked at me speculatively and said, "Maybe you're right!"

The following summer, about mid-July, who comes walking toward me but Dr. Morrow and his girlfriend. "We'd like to make reservations for dinner and dancing this evening and I'd like to pay you now."

I looked down at her left hand but there was no ring on it. So he had taken my advice. They came a few times during that summer.

The following summer, Dr. Morrow approached me with a strange looking woman. I asked, "Who is your new girl friend?" "I'm the same one, Mrs. K," she answered. "It's just that I'm wearing a wig. I had chemotherapy and this is the result. But don't worry, the doctors say that I'll recover, that I'll be well and able again. That's why we're here for dinner and dancing again."

During the winter, my master of ceremonies called me and said, "I just called to tell you that Dr. Morrow had a heart attack and passed away. I wonder if you'll have your 'available woman' back again?"

MR. MAYS

For many years I operated bungalow colony in conjunction with the Aladdin, my summer resort hotel in the Catskill Mountains. It was July 1st, in the early sixties. The man in front of my registration desk seemed distressed and unhappy.

"You mean you have no bungalow available? My wife, who practically lives in a wheel chair, is exhausted." I said, "Can you tell me a little about your problem?" He looked thoughtfully at me and then said, "We live in Florida and I sent out a few inquiries to several bungalow colonies who advertised. One day a woman called and said she would like to discuss the summer rental of a bungalow. We made an appointment and she showed us some glowing pictures, plus one particular picture of a bungalow which she thought would be ideal for us. My wheel chair wife would enjoy the view. Her raves had us sold, and she persuaded us to give her half of the bungalow rent. We were so happy to be spared looking further. When we arrived at the bungalow colony we were sure we were at the wrong place. From the glowing pictures to that dump was unbelievable, and there was that same woman sitting at her desk and I asked, 'Where is that beautiful bungalow you showed us on your pictures? For this place we gave you so much money?'" The woman jumped up and said, "What are you talking about? To me this place is beautiful. I have been here for many years and the same people keep coming back." I looked at her for a moment and said, "I hope you will be here for many more years, but I would like you to return my deposit."

"Don't be foolish, my good man. My season is on already. I reserved this bungalow for you and it's too late now for me to re-rent it at this late date. I cannot return your deposit." "You old crow," I said, "I wouldn't stay here if you paid me. Your place is disgusting looking and uninviting."

"So here I am. What can you do for me?" "Not very much" I answered. "You need a special bungalow with no steps. All my bungalows are occupied, but I have a suggestion. I have a fairly large room in a building close to the hotel. There are eight large rooms all on one floor, with only one step up into the building. It has a covered front porch where you can sit and relax. The room is carpeted, heated, and air-conditioned. Linen and maid service are provided and you can enjoy all of our facilities—indoor and outdoor pools, plus nightly entertainment in our night club. So you see you have bungalow and hotel services thrown in."

Mr. Mays viewed the room and was pleased that it had a stall shower, which was a necessity. He decided to take it and moved right in. A few days later, when I met Mr. Mays, he said, "We feel a little cramped in one room on account of the wheel chair but we are making the best of it."

The strange part of our relationship was that Mr. Mays had the same complaint every day. It was an onerous job taking full care of an adult baby. He had to wash, dress, take his wife to a special toilet provided by Medicare, and feed her. He got rid of a little steam by talking to me. He really had a full time job. In his free time I saw him relaxing on the front porch. He also had to undress his wife and put her to bed. He then got into his car to do the shopping. Occasionally they went out to dinner, but carrying a body into a car and then to a restaurant was a tax on an elderly man's strength.

One day I passed Mrs. Mays when she was sitting alone. I remarked to her that this was the first time I saw her sitting alone. She smiled and said, "Quite a number of years ago, Mr. Mays became suddenly very ill. The doctors shook their heads and said, 'We don't know. His condition is very serious.' I never left his side. I took care of him day and night. I even slept next to him in case he needed something. After a good many weeks, Mr. Mays began to improve. Then he was fully recovered and he thanked me and said he didn't know how to repay me. I thought awhile and said, 'Maybe someday I may become seriously ill, although I doubt it. But in case I do, let's make some agreement that you will take care of me as I have done for you.' We made a solemn pact, with Mr. Mays's hand on his heart. Little did I know then that I would become as helpless as I am now. Mr. Mays has kept his promise faithfully and has never let me down. As a matter of fact, he's doing too much right now and it troubles me." As I saw Mr. Mays approaching, I left her alone.

Mr. Mays's attitude began to change. Every time he saw me he spat out, "I never was so uncomfortable. I get so tired, I don't know what to do." He really upset me. I had made every effort to please him and make him comfortable: He didn't have to clean their room and his bed was made every day. It got to the point that I avoided Mr. Mays. I was even praying that he would leave.

Toward the beginning of September most of my regulars had signed up for the following season. When I looked up from my desk one day, there was Mr. Mays staring down at me. "Now what are you doing here, Mr. Mays? Soon you'll be leaving and I'll be missing your complaints."

"Did I really complain? Well, I had become really uncomfortable and wanted to make you uncomfortable, too."

"So what are you doing here? You should be packing to leave, and I won't miss you."

Mr. Mays opened his eyes wide in surprise. "You sound as if you really mean what you are saying. I really came here to see what you can offer me for next year. If you give me something I can be happy with, I will be eternally grateful. We both love it here; my wife has been especially happy with everything. We made good friends, we love your shows, and we love the grounds."

You could have knocked me down with a fly swatter.

I eventually accommodated Mr. Mays with a large, comfortable bungalow, which had a covered porch, also near the main building. There was a little road in front of his building and everyone who passed by the Mays stopped to chat, which delighted them.

Mr. and Mrs. Mays occupied that bungalow for three consecutive years and had renewed for a fourth year. During the month of May the following year, Mr. Mays called me to reserve a room with a private bath, near them, for a nurse. "Is Mrs. Mays so ill?" I asked. There was silence at the other end of the line. Then Mr. Mays said in a sad voice, "No, the nurse is for me. I can't work the way I used to. I feel worn out."

About the middle of the next month, June, Mrs. Mays called me. "Mrs. K, I have sad news for you. I am sorry to inform you that Mr. Mays passed away suddenly. His heart just gave out. I'm now in a nursing home. No one in the family wanted to take care of me. I can't really blame them. It was too much for

Mr. Mays. It's too late to regret my selfishness. I should have insisted on some help for him. Sometimes we are just stupid and blind. I'm calling you to return our deposit. I need every dollar I can lay my hands on. I now have to be careful with my finances. I want to thank you for the most wonderful years of my life at the Aladdin. I made many friends there and I hope they will not forget me. God bless you all!"

After that call, I just sat and reflected. This was the second time such an incident occurred here. The first time, the husband lasted a little longer, but as I watched the husband looking more and more peaked every year, I realized how difficult it was for a man to try to give full-time care to a woman. The first man's wife was a little more demanding. He had to carry her to the car and escort her to the beauty parlor and take her more often to dine out. An unsung hero. I can say the same for another hero. His wife developed Alzheimer's disease and her husband took care of her so that no one was aware of her condition. He would take walks with her, holding her by the arm and pretending he was talking to her. By the end of the summer, the poor man was so exhausted that he approached me and told me of his plight. He said he had decided to call the hotel quits and was leaving all his cooking equipment behind him. He knew it was the end of the line for him. He wiped the tears from his eyes and said, "These were happy years for me. I came, as you know, with several couples and we enjoyed all the facilities here. You treated us as family. His voice trembled as he said "Thank you, thank you! I shall never forget the wonderful years we all spent here!"

When I was alone, I wept, not for him but for myself. How green was my valley!

MY IRISHMAN

Soon after the death of my husband, Abe, after many seasons of shutting down completely after Labor Day, I decided to keep one building open through the winter. We called it the "Winter House," and it was identified by that name even when converted to a place for summer rental. In addition to the bedrooms, I equipped the house with a kitchen. It was my intention to rent the building after the summer season, and that is how I met Arthur Shea.

Mr. Shea impressed me as well mannered, a gentleman. When he expressed an interest in renting a room with the kitchen for the fall and winter, I considered it. He clinched the deal when he insisted upon paying two months in advance. Because the Winter House was directly across the road from my year-round residence, I saw Mr. Shea often. When I sat outside to enjoy the mid-day sun or read, he would sometimes join me. We discussed our respective trades. He was the supervisor of the local prison and had lots of stories to tell. I shared with him the idiosyncrasies of my guests. I found him pleasant, intelligent, charming, and before long I considered him a friend.

Arthur—before long we were addressing each other by first names—eventually asked if he could do things for me. He offered to pick up my mail, shop for groceries, run errands for me. I told him I liked to do things for myself. I preferred independence and enjoyed performing my chores. He seemed to accept that and respect it. Our friendship continued to grow as we exchanged intimacies as well as stories. I wasn't entirely surprised when he invited me dinner, but I declined.

Arthur was a tall Irishman and I am a little Jewish woman. Better just to remain companions. However, Arthur was persistent. "If you don't want to come to dinner, how about coming to a bar with me?" Can you imagine a little old Jewish woman sitting at a bar? I laughed and asked him that question. "Well," he said, "I had to try something. I enjoy your company and thought we ought to do something more than 'schmooze'."

One day Arthur asked if he could take some pictures of me, and I allowed him to do so. Then he asked me if I would invite him into my home. I opened my door and said, "You can sit here in my living room and we can talk."

Arthur said, "I am really attracted to you. I have been from the first day that I set eyes on you. And it wasn't here at the hotel. At the post office I heard you laughing and discussing some topic with the postmistress. You charmed me. Your voice soothed me. I felt good and warm all over as I never felt before. Believe it or not, I had a feeling of having always known you. When you left, I asked the postmistress who you were. I was shocked to learn that you were a hotelkeeper. How do you meet a hotelkeeper? I thought about that for a while and then decided to go over and get the lay of the land. When I got to the hotel I saw a sign 'Efficiencies to Rent'. That gave me an idea. That's when I met you and you showed me around. I still felt the same way I did at the post office so I rented the unit for two months. I couldn't believe that I could be that dumb, but there I was with an apartment on my hands and, strangest of all, I felt quite happy and content. I said to myself, 'You must be nuts,' but I was satisfied with my deal. Every time I saw you sitting outside, I made a beeline to your side. I just wanted to be near you and surprised myself by asking to help you with any errand, to go to the post office, to the supermarket, anything, but you always refused. Now I'm a little embarrassed. Would you care to continue your friendship with me?"

What do you answer to a question like that? I studied Arthur for a moment and then asked, "How old are you, Arthur?"

He said, "I am 66 years old."

"Well," I said, "I'm 76, ten years older than you. I am an old woman." I thought that would make a difference and I needn't get involved. Would you believe his answer? He said, "Biology and physiology are two different things. I feel that you are younger than I am. You have lots of pep; you have a wonderful outlook on life; you are able to make good decisions and you never seem depressed."

I had a feeling that he wanted to embrace me, or more. I suddenly found something that needed my attention in the room. Then Arthur said, "In a week or so I'll be leaving. I have to make arrangements for my retirement from the prison and decide how to arrange my life now that I won't have a job. This is a difficult time for me." He left some unspoken words hanging in the air. And I thought to myself "Don't I have enough troubles already?"

The next day Arthur joined me as usual and we talked and acted as if nothing had passed between us. A few days later, Arthur said he was leaving the next morning but hoped that we could continue our friendship. I had to say something, so I said, "Any time you're in the area, I'll be happy to have you visit me."

The next day Arthur left very early in the morning so I didn't see him. He said his home was in Avoca, three hundred miles away. That was quite a trip.

About a week later, I received a package from the post office. When I opened it, there was a small, pretty ladies' watch on a gold chain. Undaunted Arthur. The following week, I received a box of embroidered handkerchiefs. I was being wooed in earnest. As long as he was so far away, I was safe.

About two weeks later, Arthur called and said he was having a reunion with his buddies at the prison and asked me to reserve a room for him for one night. I did, but he spent the whole afternoon with me. He told me that he had a lovely home in Avoca and also had a luxurious log cabin in the woods for the summertime. He said if it weren't for the hotel, maybe he'd have a chance. He also showed me a picture of his room, and my pictures were on his dresser.

Finally I asked him if he had ever been married. He grimaced and said he made a hasty marriage when he was inducted into the army. When he came out there was no living with the shrew, and it ended in divorce. Since that time he was content to live a quiet, single existence. Now he wasn't happy living alone any more. Something was missing. Since he was leaving the next day, he asked me for his bill. I felt hateful for charging him, but maybe he would despise me for the charge.

A week later, Arthur called again. I told him I was leaving for my vacation in Florida. There was silence on the other end for a minute or so, and then he said, "I hope you don't fall in love with any man you go fishing with." I laughed. "Arthur, old ladies don't go fishing and I'm staying with my sister. We find things to do. We attend her club meetings; we buy tickets for shows her organization runs; we attend dinners to raise money for charitable organizations. In general we keep ourselves occupied. No love affairs."

A short time after I returned home, Arthur called. He hesitated a moment and then he said, "When I visited you last I wanted to kiss you with all my heart, but I was scared. Now I'm scared, but I'm calling to ask you to marry me. I'm accustomed to running a house and I'll take good care of you." At my age! Woe is me!

"Arthur," I said, "I'll think about it but don't count on it." A short time later Arthur called and begged "Please come and visit me. No strings attached. If it bothers you, I have a lock on every bedroom door. I just want you to see my home and I'll prepare a lovely dinner for you."

Was it worth traveling three hundred miles? Maybe a hundred miles might have been short enough to encourage me to drive out, but three hundred miles? I didn't care for him that much. I didn't hear from him after that. A year passed, and I thought I would send him a New Year's card to show him that I did not forget him.

The letter was returned, 'Deceased.' In shock, I realized that he must have known that he was dying but he hadn't wanted me to come out of sympathy. He wanted 'friend to friend,' and the fantasy of more.

ON AGING

It was the Rosh Hashanah Holiday and I received a reservation with a deposit for a single room with semi-private bath. A very kindly elderly man showed up and I checked him in.

Several hours later the hotel received a hysterical call from the single woman in the adjoining room. She had been a guest with us before.

"What's wrong with you people? I may be a single woman but if you have to put a man in the adjoining room, why didn't you put at least a single man whose company I can enjoy? You put an old man next door who doesn't close his door and walks around with no pants on. I'm not interested in such sights and I want you to do something about this. I have no intention of suffering. I came here to enjoy the holiday."

I conferred with my secretary and we decided that the best thing to do was to give this man a room with a private bath to avoid further trouble. We had an eight-room building in front of the main house, with just one step up. All rooms were on one floor.

We moved Mr. Engel to this room and he seemed content. When his valise arrived, he just opened it on the floor of his closet and proceeded to hang his clothes, one by one, from the floor on to a hanger. We left him in peace—mission accomplished!

I generally don't leave the office until the night man comes in to take over. Suddenly a hostile group of people came marching in, fire in their eyes. "How do you expect us to get into our rooms when the front door is locked?"

At no time was this door locked. My secretary and I figured that our lovely old gentleman must have locked the door before going to his room. How to get in? I didn't have a key, because no key was ever needed! Banging on the door was no use. Our friend must have been fast asleep. We tried throwing pebbles at his window to wake him up. Throw today, throw tomorrow. No answer. Our night man had to go to the storeroom and bring out a ladder, which he placed in front of Mr. Engel's window. After banging for a few minutes, he finally awakened our guest and explained the situation. Mr. Engel put his pants on and opened the door. All quiet on the western front, or so we thought. After breakfast, Mr. Engel's tablemates collected at the front desk. "Either you take that old man off our table or change our seats! We can't stand the way he slobbers over his food. We came here to enjoy the holiday and we don't mean to suffer."

Now I really had a problem. How to get in touch with relatives? I sat down with Mr. Engel and after much questioning I got the phone number of his son. Fortunately, I was able to contact him and in a few hours Mr. Engel's son appeared.

This is what we learned: Mr. Engel, the father, had been a very successful businessman and had always managed to take care of himself. However, in recent months he had been neglecting himself, often omitting meals. The family decided that the best thing was to place Mr. Engel in a retirement home where he would enjoy privacy and be served his meals and have an attendant to help take care of his needs.

This plan seemed to be working out very satisfactorily, but Mr. Engel still felt he was master of his own destiny and while in the home, he decided to make a reservation for himself independently. He wanted to meet other people and show that he could take care of himself. So he sat down, wrote a lovely letter with a check and sent it off to us. He could still carry on an intelligent conversation; he had a checking account; he had several hours to himself for his own recreation. His sudden disappearance occurred with no indication to his caretakers that he intended to leave and no hint of where he was going.

It is sad that suddenly a person changes from an independent citizen to someone who needs attention along the way to helplessness. Each person undergoes aging in different ways. Let us pray that we can always be masters of our own destiny.

Mr. Engel's son took his father home, thanking us, and we proceeded with our daily routines. I couldn't help wondering, who will be next?

MOTHER LOVE

She was a middle-aged woman who worked in an agency that supplied entertainment to hotels and organizations. Many of the acts were sent to the Catskill Mountains' summer resorts that did a great business entertaining their guests. Spending so much time in the office, she became acquainted with most of the actors and they always greeted her warmly.

After so many years, an idea was gradually forming in her mind. The commission paid to the agency was greater than her salary. She and her husband had to keep working to take care of their daily needs and also to save for the future. Why not try to form some arrangement to do some of this business herself? She had the names and phone numbers of entertainers as well as the places that booked them. She consulted with her husband and after much discussion, he decided that it would be a good idea to talk to hotel owners and feel them out.

A few hotelkeepers sympathized with such an arrangement, especially since the rates for these acts would be much lower than those the agency charged. Thus began a new business. Little by little, Bertha, the agent, contacted acts which she knew were good, and they agreed to try her. Slowly Bertha gained a following and both she and her husband thrived. While not making a fortune, they both loved each other dearly and were thrilled whenever they made a deposit.

Bertha usually had her dinners at my hotel, since I gave her a special rate and never said anything when she packed two or three sandwiches in her bag for her husband. For a number of years they led a contented and happy life. Their savings account was growing. They had a son living in California who was a successful songwriter and he kept calling them to come to California where he would buy a home for them where they could retire in peace. Bertha and husband felt that the time was not ripe and they would consider it at some future date. A short time later the grandchildren called. They were compelling. So Bertha and husband disposed of what they couldn't take and moved to California to be united with their family.

One day their son, Howard, told them he had great news. Two friends were planning to open a show on Broadway. Since the son was a professional songwriter and his friends had a script for a musical, they had decided to go to New York and seek their fortune.

Bertha heard this with a sinking heart. "Why do you have to go to New York, my son? You don't want to be the richest man on earth. You're making a good living here. Be happy here."

"That's all right for you older folks. But we have to make progress, we're young. And we're leaving for New York next week." "I can't stop you, son. God be with you. I'll pray for you."

A week later Howard was established in a penthouse apartment near Lincoln Center. Now began the hunt for a theater, which cost a king's ransom, and haunting the agencies for proper performers. It took weeks of rehearsal plus a tremendous amount for salaries, a whole lot more money than planned. They had no backer and their savings diminished.

Soon came the day for opening night. All three men were nervous and high strung. Would the show go over? What would the critics' reaction be? Many times Howard remembered his mother's words. Why didn't he listen? His former successes had turned his head.

The three friends spread throughout the theater. The attendance could have been much better. What they thought would be a great success turned out to be a failure. They were crushed. The show closed the second week and three heartbroken men returned home practically penniless.

What was Howard to do now? His mother was in the hospital and she was the only one he could turn to. When he went to visit her, he sat by her bed, speechless.

"What is it, Howard? I can see by your face that things didn't turn out the way you expected. How can I help you?"

Howard wet his lips. "I came to beg to borrow some money from you so that I can get back on my feet. I hope in due time that I may be able to return your loan."

"It isn't necessary to promise anything. I'm your mother and I am going to give you all the money dad and I have saved up. Bring me a paper and pen and I will close out my accounts to you."

"I have no alternative, mother. There is no other person I can turn to. You can rest assured that I hope to return everything you are giving me and much more."

A few days later the hospital informed Howard that his mother had passed away.

The shock and grief overcame Howard and it took weeks before he could even talk intelligently to anyone, even his wife. He just sat dejectedly with his head in his hands and quietly wept. As he sat, words kept repeating themselves in his mind.

After all, he was a very successful and famous songwriter. The words kept repeating themselves and subconsciously he already had a song in his mind. This was so astonishing to him that he fell on his knees and prayed: "Dear God, let me come back and justify my dear mother. I shall do penance all my life." The song he wrote:

> Oh mother of mine
> How do I pine
> In my body
> My heart is bleeding
> For a lost one
> I wasn't heeding
> Round and round I go
> Where it will end
> I do not know
> Sing a song
> It won't be long
> Till my heart will ease
> I pray to God please.

Although the words were very sentimental, Howard's melody was soft, beautiful, soothing and haunting, a song that only a troubled soul could compose. People who heard Howard's lament felt a kinship in their hearts and subconsciously kept humming the melody, feeling the sadness expressed by this talented songwriter. It turned out to be a smashing success. So in the end Howard's mother, poor Bertha (or should I say rich Bertha) still took care of her child, even in death. It made Howard a more attentive father and a more charitable man. Not so for Howard's father. He mourned for his loving wife and turned to the synagogue for whatever comfort he could find. It gave him a sad joy when Howard presented the synagogue with a memorial Torah in Bertha's name.

Neither one ever found out that Bertha had committed suicide. There was no one to stop her. Oh Bertha, poor Bertha, why did you despair? Why did you send *me* the terrible letter that arrived after all your troubles were over?

A FAREWELL TO MR. McCORMACK

A few days ago, I was standing outside when I noticed a car stop near me. A tall man got out. He walked slowly over to me and said, "If it isn't Mrs. Komito! Am I glad to see you!" He looked familiar but I couldn't place him. His eyes were sad and he looked ill.

"I'm sure I know you but I don't remember your name."

"I don't blame you, Mrs. K. I know I've changed a great deal. I'm a very sick man but I had to visit you. I am Mr. McCormack, the Health and Building inspector from the Monticello District. At least I was. I'm retired now. For the past few weeks, thoughts of you have never left my mind, so I finally got out of bed and got into my car. I now live in Middletown but I remember my visits to your hotel. I always looked forward to seeing you but you never knew why. As soon as you saw me, you put your hands on your hips and exclaimed, 'I knew something bad was going to happen to me today and here you are! Now what are you here for?'

"Mrs. Komito, it was the friendly sarcasm in your voice that tickled my risibles. When I told you that I had orders to go through the main house to make sure no one could occupy the top floor, that the hallways had to be boarded up, your eyes had a twinkle in them and you said softly, 'Go on up if you have to. I only hope you can't find your way down!'

"I really got a kick out of your sarcasm but never felt offended. As a matter of fact, I looked forward to your sallies. They braced me for the rest of the day. I am a terminally ill man and, believe it or not, I keep smiling to myself at all the times you twitted me. And then I said to myself—I've been pretty tough with this little lady and I must tell her how I feel about my visits. I'm a dying man but I must pull myself together and talk to her once more. This time you don't have to worry that I am going to give you some violations to sign. I'm here because I want to get you out of my mind by squaring myself with you. You are the only person that I ever looked forward to. You just put me in a good humor. Many times after one of your speeches, I ran into the building so you shouldn't see and just burst into laughter. I just wanted you to forgive me and to tell you that I really enjoyed your company and felt it was only proper to tell you while I am still alive."

We were sitting on two chairs outside my apartment and when I looked up at Mr. McCormack, the tears were slowly falling. They brought tears to my eyes also. I placed my hand on top of his and squeezed it sympathetically. "My heart aches for both of us."

"I'm very tired now but I had to get rid of you (this with a twinkle). Now I must go. I really enjoyed sitting here with you. Maybe we will meet in heaven."

"Oh no," I exclaimed, "God will never let me run a hotel in heaven and be harassed by inspectors like you. So don't let it worry you."

"That's what I like about you." He bent down and kissed me, saying, "This time you have scored!" So saying, he got into his car and I watched as his car drove away into the blue sky yonder.

STATE OF NEW YORK

DEPARTMENT OF HEALTH

HOLLIS S. INGRAHAM, M.D.
COMMISSIONER
DISTRICT HEALTH OFFICER

MONTICELLO SUB-DISTRICT OFFICE
6 Prince Street, Monticello, N. Y. 12701

MICHAEL LIPARI, M. 0.

August 10, 1971
Re: Aladdin Hotel
Town of Fallsburg

Mr. Abraham Komito, Sec.
Levbourne Realty Co., Inc.
Woodbourne, New York 12788

Dear Sir:

A complete inspection of the above mentioned temporary residence was made on August 2, 1971, by Mr. J. McCormick, a representative of this Department.

At the time of the inspection your establishment was operating in substantial conformity with the provisions of the State Sanitary Code.

Your continued cooperation in the maintenance of safe sanitary conditions will be appreciated.

Very truly Yours

Gerald Lieber, P.E.
Sanitary Engineer

A DESCRIPTION OF OUR MASTER OF CEREMONIES

I know you all love your Emcee, Murray Waxman, and you enjoy his shows and his humor, but do you know the real Murray? You would, if you saw him at night when he goes to bed. First, he takes off his wig, then he removes one leg and hangs it at the foot of his bed so he can find it in the morning. Then he takes out his glass eye and places it on the night table beside his bed so that it can watch him when he's asleep. This is the real Murray.

You can now see him in the Rogue's Gallery in Madam Taussud's Wax Museum. Here he is created in wax, standing on one leg and waving the other in his other hand. His wig hangs dangerously over one ear, and his glass eye is still in his head but facing in another direction.

Murray occupies a special place here since he is the center of everyone's visit. A depressed person goes away full of smiles. However, there is now an added price for this attraction since the carpet has been worn away in front of his statue.

I just want all of you to know what a brave person you have in your midst. Long may he wave!

And let's let Murray talk for himself. He always does, and we're the better for listening.

MY FIRST CATSKILL
ENGAGEMENT
BY MURRAY B. WAXMAN

My history in the Catskill Mountains began in the summer of 1931. I auditioned with a Jewish theatrical company and was accepted immediately. Our first job as a company began at the Grand View Hotel in Hurleyville, across the road from another hotel named Rubel's Mansion. Louis Weiss, together with his wife, Florence, headed our company. We were a group of six actors and I was selected to play the "Young Lover" as I had a substantial singing voice. This vagabond company was constantly arguing and very combative. Things became intolerable; they reached a point where no one spoke to anyone else. One day, the owner, Sara Seldon, came to the rehearsal and, seeing and hearing our complaints, fired us on the spot!

During our two-week gig at the hotel, I had noticed an elderly gentleman with a black suit and a black derby to match. Upon hearing of our being fired, he asked me if I would like to work as a social director at his hotel across the street, namely, Rubel's Mansion. Of course, I accepted the offer, which was for $2.00 a week. I would entertain the guests at lunch and at dinner. In between I had to burnish the silverware—all for $2.00 a week! And oh yes, I had to dance with the "yentas" in the casino at night after the show. These were my commitments—all for $2.00 a week.

My sleeping quarters were on the porch, surrounded by a tarpaulin on a rickety old cot that was broken on both ends. I didn't complain for I was doing what I loved most and that was entertaining, singing and telling jokes. I must say I did a helluva job. As the season progressed I became very adept at doing my job and I became a fixture in the hotel, or so I thought.

The following event took place on Friday of Labor Day Weekend. I was approached by the owner, who said, "Young man, you are fired." "Why?" I asked in a voice loud enough to be heard in Fallsburgh. The owner told me that he needed my broken cot for a guest for the weekend. Very much taken aback, I asked him, "If I can find a place to sleep, could I finish out the Labor Day weekend?" He agreed. So for three nights I slept on a chair in the lobby. Boy was I cramped.

I vowed that I would never again take a job for $2.00 a week.

From 1931 to the present day, I have become a legend in the Catskills. *The New York Post* featured my accomplishments in a full-page story. The Gannett *Newspapers* and *The Middletown Herald* all did two pages on my history. I am now partially retired. I still do my 'shtick' in Florida and am very much in demand. But I will never forget my first paying job, if you could call it that, at $2.00 a week.

THE GLATT WOK

Originally the Catskill vacation spots were all farmhouses. When I was fifteen, my mother sent me to a farm owned by one of her friends, to recuperate from an illness. This was the beginning of the hotel idea. Outdoors, there were cows on the premises. Inside, the dining room consisted of a few very long tables with benches for seats. The table was laden with milk, bread, rolls, butter, sugar, sweet cream, and more. A waiter brought several boxes of dry cereal and dumped them on the table. He then presented three wire baskets: soft, medium, hard-boiled eggs. He dropped off the orders and went on to the next table.

From these beginnings, small hotels gradually sprang up, and later large ones. A modern hotel boasted rooms with semi-private bath on each end of the hallway, with bath on the floor for the middle rooms. You were looked upon as wealthy if you occupied a semi-private room. After dinner the guests sat around in the lobby. If someone had a harmonica, there was singing in the lobby, or there was a dance exhibition by a talented woman; a joke-teller was a treat. For other amusements there was a mock marriage or a hayride. Most guests participated and good time was usually enjoyed by all. A far cry from the elaborate stage settings and professional entertainment of our future. Our pool was the Neversink River with wooden steps leading to the beach. The water was always icy. The inn-keeper quivered when he conducted a guest to this swimming hole. "What, no pool?" It was a question always to be dreaded. We knew that sooner or later we'd have to build one. It was either do or die—and we did. We had no choice.

Nothing is static. If that generation complained, the next deserted us. It wanted to see what the rest of the world looked like. The children were sent to summer camps and the parents decided to either cruise or fly. This put a damper on the hotel business and most of the old hotels gave up. The mountains were in the doldrums. To repeat, nothing is static. New people appeared on the horizon. These were ultra religious Jews and they had heard about the wonders of the Catskills: good fresh air, cool evenings, and good facilities for the children. The children were their main concern. Every family had from six to ten children. There had to be plenty of space for them. They had to find colonies where they would be welcome and where they could associate with their own kind. The Jewish immigrants had found the ideal vacation land for their needs. These ultra-religious people were following God's commands to be fruitful and multiply as the sands of the earth, and this they did.

Now there was a rebirth of the Catskills. These families were filling up all the vacant bungalows with their own people. Husbands left their families during the week and came up for the weekends, duplicating the original vacationers. Wherever you went, you came across these Glatt people. They came to stay and the towns began to look active and busy. New life had been injected. Glatt shops opened everywhere to accommodate these people's needs.

Recently, the new owner of my old hotel, which had grown to include over a hundred bungalows, became a venturesome and decided to let her son-in-law open a 'Glatt Wok,' a Chinese dining room and a restaurant, similar to the one he owned in Brooklyn. Since most of their guests lived in the same area and spent the summers in the Catskills, he did not lack customers. He had lovely Chinese waitresses and people enjoyed a 'change of pace' with different, tasty Chinese fare.

Now it seems to be a success, a good business every day. Gradually, without fanfare, Glatt is becoming American. Today at the beginning of the 21st century, music is piped into the dining rooms. It wouldn't be surprising if dancing became accepted. The economy of the country depends on its young people. They are the spenders who will inherit the earth. Entertainment? Who knows? Strange things are happening! Cycles repeat. God bless America. God bless 'Glatt Wok.'